Department of Health

TRIALS
and
TRIBULATIONS

Returning Children from Local Authority Care
to their Families

Elaine Farmer   Roy Parker

LONDON : HMSO

Contents

Acknowledgements

The research described in this book was made possible by financial support from the Department of Health and Social Security under its former 'small grants' scheme. We are grateful for this assistance and also for the help of our research liaison officer Dr Carolyn Davies.

We are particularly indebted to the four local authorities and their staff who enabled the research to be undertaken. It is never easy to have one's work scrutinised by outsiders but despite that we were accorded every facility and met with kindness, co-operation and a keen interest in what we were doing.

We are also extremely grateful to the parents and social workers who talked to us at great length. They provided the vivid and personal commentaries that were so valuable in leavening what would otherwise have been a study wholly dependent upon records.

Fiona Crummay usefully assisted us with part of the data collection. Many colleagues at Bristol and elsewhere have commented on our drafts but we are particularly grateful to members of the Dartington Social Research Unit, to Frank Loughran, Phyllida Parsloe, Gwynn Davis, Jean Packman, June Thoburn, Jane Aldgate, Jane Rowe and Valerie Bramwell. In addition we would like to thank Michael Little who gave us such valuable and unstinting assistance with the statistical analysis.

Finally, we would like to thank Pat Lees for the generous assistance she has given us throughout the study and in particular for the meticulous care and outstanding skill with which she typed the material.

PART I

The Background

CHAPTER 1

Introduction

Courts have long exercised the power to remove delinquent children[1] from the care of their parents. Children were imprisoned or transported together with adults. It was not until the middle decades of the last century that they could be committed to industrial or reformatory schools instead. Likewise, it was not until then that younger children could be sent to industrial schools because they were considered to be in danger of embarking upon a life of crime as a result of the harmful influence of their parents, their associates or their surroundings.[2] Other grounds for committing children to industrial schools were added over the years; most notably that they were in moral danger; that they were beyond the control of their parents, and that they had failed repeatedly to attend school.

Two important enactments in 1889 established other grounds and ways in which children could be removed from their parents' care.[3] The first enabled courts to commit children who had been abused by their parents to the care of a 'fit person'. Later, fit person orders were extended to cover cases of neglect as well as those circumstances that could also lead to a child being made the subject of an industrial school order. Fit person orders and approved school orders (as the industrial and reformatory school orders became after 1933) were integrated in 1969 as the care orders of today. Although the grounds for making them have been substantially modified by the 1989 Children Act[4] courts continue to have the power to commit certain children to the care of local authorities until they are 18.

The other significant piece of legislation that was passed in 1889 gave boards of guardians the power, without recourse to the courts, to assume

[3]

parental rights in respect of a child who had been taken into their care on a voluntary basis if they considered that the parents were no longer willing, able or fit to exercise those rights. That provision has continued virtually unchanged to the present (albeit other authorities superseded the guardians) and is only now to disappear with the implementation of the 1989 Children Act.

We make these brief historical points in order to emphasise the assortment of circumstances in which it has been possible to remove children from the care of their parents when their well-being was considered to be endangered. Furthermore, for a considerable part of this history it was assumed that removal should be long-term, and even when children grew up steps were taken to keep them from what was frequently regarded as detrimental contact with their parents. Admittedly, there were provisions for parents to apply to the courts for orders to be discharged, but only a trickle of applications was made and even fewer were successful.

The historical context within which children came to be compulsorily removed from home was not conducive to the development of policies or practices for their early restoration to their families. The first notable shift in that direction occurred in the industrial school system soon after the turn of the century. The Home Office became increasingly concerned about the number of children in the schools and about the cost to the Exchequer that this entailed. The licensing system was not being used as soon or as frequently as intended. Schools were disinclined in principle to release children early but were also reluctant to do so for financial reasons. However, changes in the way in which the schools were financed, combined with stronger central government control of licensing policy, led to more and more children being released under supervision prior to the expiry of their orders. Since they could be recalled whilst on licence they were in effect allowed home (or into residential employment) 'on trial'.[5]

Apart from these developments in what became the approved school system after 1933, little progress was made in the early rehabilitation with their families of children who had been committed to care. Typically, they remained in care until their orders expired at 16 (and later at 18). However, the establishment of local authority children's departments in 1948, together with the wider remit of the child care inspectorate of the Home Office and the gradual emergence of an identifiable profession of child care, helped to encourage the reorientation of policy; but developments were slow and uneven. Many children remained in care for unnecessarily long periods[6] and this was especially true for those who had been committed to care by the courts. Indeed, until the Family Allowances and National Insurance Act of 1956[7] it was uncertain whether it was legally possible for local authorities to return children committed to their care 'home on trial', although some children's departments had adopted the practice. However, that raised the question of whether or not the families were then entitled to resume drawing the family allowance; hence the location in social security legislation of the measure that finally made it clear that placements home on trial were legally permitted and that family allowances could be paid to the parents.

However, although the term 'home on trial' was being used in children's departments during the 1950s it was not possible to determine the scale of the practice until 1960 when, for the first time, local authorities were required to furnish this information to the Home Office children's department. Their returns revealed that in that year in England and Wales some 2,000 children who were subject to fit person orders were home on trial; that is, 10 per cent of all committed children. By 1964 it was possible to add in those children who were subject to parental rights resolutions but allowed to be at home. These two categories amounted to about 4,000 children home on trial, or 13 per cent of the relevant total. By 1971, when the children's departments were absorbed into the newly-created local social services departments, that proportion had risen to 21 per cent.[8] Clearly, the placement 'home on trial' of children who were compulsorily in care had become a well used practice and one that resembled the licensing system in the approved schools.

However, there were two important differences between the systems. In the first place the licensing of approved school children (most of whom were young offenders) was for a fixed period, after which supervision ceased. By contrast, children who had been committed to the care of a local authority (for example because they had been abused or neglected) and were then allowed home on trial could remain in that position until the order expired on their eighteenth birthday. Secondly, when a child was released on licence from an approved school it was plain that it was he or she who was on trial for their good behaviour. For those who were permitted to go home on trial by children's departments the situation was more complicated. Some of these children who were offenders or who had failed to go to school might certainly have been regarded as being 'on trial'. In the case of those who had been neglected or abused, however, it was clear that it was the behaviour of the parents towards the child which was on trial.

These differences became blurred after the implementation of the 1969 Children and Young Persons Act. In 1971 all the children within the approved school system (12,300 of them) were transferred to the care of the new social services departments. As a result, the number of children 'in care' was instantly enlarged, both by those who were resident in the schools and by those who were on licence. This latter group, which numbered 4,800, was immediately added to the total of those who were in care but home on trial. By 1972, therefore, there were some 15,250 children home on trial[9] or almost 30 per cent of those compulsorily in local authority care. However, the growth (which continued to a peak of nearly 19,000 in 1978 before beginning to decline) was not attributable solely to the transfer of approved school children on licence. More committed children in general were now placed home on trial.

One of the reasons for this may be found in the new care orders that were introduced by the 1969 Act. Whereas the former approved school orders were for a fixed period (typically two to three years) care orders remained in place until the child reached the age of eighteen unless they were previously discharged. The supervision at home (or elsewhere) of approved school children came to an end fairly quickly and automatically; nobody had to do anything. For a care order to be discharged, however, an application needed to be made to the court, evidence assembled and time set aside. In the early hectic days of the new social services departments such work was liable to receive a low priority and, as a result, children who were home on trial could well have remained in that status for long periods, thereby swelling the number so enumerated. Gradually, as more children who were home on trial had their care orders discharged (and more had them discharged sooner), the number of children home on trial fell—but not to any significant extent until 1983. Even so, in 1987 there were still some 10,000 children home on trial in England and Wales, a figure that accounted for about a fifth of all children subject to compulsory care.[10]

Thus, the placement back home of children in respect of whom a local authority continues to have parental responsibility has been, and remains, a widespread practice. It raises innumerable questions about when such placements should be made and how long it should be before the orders are discharged. There are profoundly important issues connected with the assessment of the risks that may be involved and therefore with the proper exercise of a local authority's responsibilities. The placements are often difficult for social workers to manage, not least because, if things go seriously wrong, the child will have to be removed and face yet further upheaval. There are also questions about expectations: lower standards of care may be tolerated when a child is placed back home on trial than would be acceptable in, say, the selection of a foster home.

Despite these and other complexities, home on trial placements have been virtually unstudied.[11] It was not known when or why children were allowed to go home, at what ages or with what intentions. Nobody knew whether, as a group, they went to parents, relatives or friends[12] or how different the households to which they returned were from the ones that they had left.

We did not know how long the placements lasted or with what degree of success. It was unclear what it meant for parents to have the day-to-day custody of their child whilst parental rights continued to be vested in a local authority; nor did we know what the children felt about it. Furthermore, as the history suggests, it was not necessarily clear who was on trial and when they had passed or failed the test.

The fact that home on trial has received so little attention in the past suggests that it was not considered particularly problematic. Certainly, it has not been developed as a special field of practice for which social workers needed to be trained. Likewise, although social services departments have fostering and adoption sections and panels to scrutinise such placements, nothing comparable has developed for placements home on trial. Similarly, although the idea of planning for permanence has attracted a great deal of attention, placement home on trial as a prelude to the permanent rehabilitation of child and family has not.

Sadly, it took the Jasmine Beckford tragedy to begin to change things.[13] She was home on trial when she died at the hands of her stepfather, having originally been committed to care for maltreatment. The report of the panel of inquiry served to emphasise the difficulties and dilemmas facing those working with families where a child was home on trial; but it also made clear that home on trial was not simply a means of dealing with older children nearing the end of their period in care.

The report also brought home the fact that there were no regulations to provide guidance and set minimum standards in respect of home on trial placements. Partly as a result of the inquiry into the case, regulations were prepared and approved by Parliament in 1988. They came into force in June, 1989,[14] marking an important recognition of both the scale and significance of such placements which were henceforth to be referred to as 'charge and control'. Detailed specifications are set out about who should make the decision to allow a child home, about who should be consulted and notified and about what is to be recorded. Rules are laid down for the pattern of supervision once a placement has been made and for its review, reassessment and, if necessary, termination.[15] Obviously, regulations do not ensure good placements or good social work; but they will, if followed with care and sensitivity, raise the standard of practice. Of equal importance, however, is the fact that they signify that the placement of a child in the charge and control of a parent, relative or friend whilst still in care is a serious matter to be approached with as much deliberation as the placement of a child with unrelated foster parents or prospective adopters.

The research that is reported in this book was conducted prior to the introduction of the Charge and Control regulations. We have, therefore, continued to employ the term 'home on trial' to describe the placements in question. The existence of research that deals with a period just before the new regulations came into force provides a benchmark against which the nature and extent of the changes in practice that follow may be assessed, although clearly other studies will be needed. We undertook this research because we believed that it was urgent to fill some of the enormous gaps in what was known about placements home on trial. We also felt that social workers and others deserved to be given whatever assistance research might be able to offer in ensuring the safe return of children to their families. It is not only that the decisions involved are difficult but that their consequences, one way or the other, can be so far-reaching. Indeed, as Jasmine Beckford's fate made plain, it may be a matter of life or death for a few children.

Notes and references

1. There has been, of course, a long-standing wardship jurisdiction as well; but, until quite recently, this has affected only a small number of children, typically from upper class families. See N. Lowe and R. White, *Wards of Court*, Butterworths, 1979.
2. For an account of these developments see, G. Rose, *Schools for Young Offenders*, Tavistock, 1967 and J. Carlebach, *Caring for Children in Trouble*, Routledge and Kegan Paul, 1970, introductory chapters.
3. The Prevention of Cruelty to Children Act, 1889 and the Poor Law (Amendment) Act, 1889.
4. For more details see Department of Health, *An Introduction to the Children Act, 1989* and R. White, P. Carr and N. Lowe, *A Guide to the Children Act, 1989*, Butterworths, 1990. The latter also contains the full text of the Act.
5. For a general history see, R.A. Parker, *Away from Home: A Short History of Provision for Separated Children*, Barnardo's, 1991.
6. This was most notably revealed in J. Rowe and L. Lambert, *Children Who Wait*, Association of British Adoption Agencies, 1973.
7. See section 5 of the 1956 Act and Home Office, *Eighth Report on the Work of the Children's Department*, HMSO, 1961; p. 18.
8. Figures derived from the annual returns to the Department of Health and Social Security, *Children in the Care of Local Authorities*.
9. These figures exclude children subject to interim care orders or remanded to care although some of them would technically have been home on trial; but the figures do include children subject to parental rights resolutions.

10. See footnote 8.
11. The one exception is June Thoburn's important study, *Captive Clients: Social Work with Families of Children Home on Trial*, Routledge and Kegan Paul, 1980.
12. The Department of Health annual return asks local authorities to specify the total number of children in care who are 'allowed to be under the charge and control of a parent, guardian, relative or friend' but does not require the number in each of these groups to be separately recorded.
13. *A Child in Trust: the Report of the Panel of Inquiry into the Circumstances Surrounding the Death of Jasmine Beckford*, London Borough of Brent, 1985.
14. Children and Young Persons, *The Accommodation of Children (Charge and Control) Regulations*, 1988; S. I. 1988, No. 2183.
15. For fuller details see, Department of Health and Welsh Office, *Handbook of Guidance: Charge and Control Placements*, 1989. These regulations will be altered and re-named when the 1989 Children Act becomes law. The changes proposed are discussed in the final chapter.

CHAPTER 2

Design: Definitions and Sources

The research was designed in two parts. The first and principal project was a case file study aimed at providing a profile of children who were home on trial, their families and their circumstances. It also traced the decisions that led to their return and the developments, practice and outcomes during the placement. The second part was intended to furnish more detailed information on a limited scale by means of a small number of interviews with a selection of families and social workers with current or recent involvement in a home on trial placement.

We adopted two principal criteria for the selection of the local authorities whose records formed the basis of the main study. First, since we wanted to provide a description of the typical uses of home on trial, we limited our selection to those authorities that clustered around the national average for the proportion of children in such placements. Secondly, in order to obtain a large enough sample of children of different kinds for each authority we restricted our choice further to those authorities with at least 200 children home on trial. Not all the authorities that satisfied these criteria were able or willing to assist us. The four upon which the study was eventually based were located in different parts of the country. Two were large metropolitan authorities, one in the Midlands and one in the North, both of them with substantial black populations. The other two were large county authorities, one in the Midlands and one in the South, and each included both rural and urban areas with small black populations in their urban centres.

The ideal design for the principal study would have been to take a population of children placed home on trial in one year and then to follow them through for two or three years. However, this was not possible as not all local authorities could provide the necessary information. We were obliged, therefore, to draw our sample from those children who were already in a home on trial placement on 31st March of a particular year, since this is the date on which local authorities make returns to the Department of Health and such information is therefore normally available. We decided to take 1984 as the year in which we drew our sample since our scrutiny of the files began in 1986 and this therefore enabled us to follow progress and developments for at least two years; that is, until 31st March, 1986.

A schedule was composed on which data could be collected. For each item of information a list of pre-coded options was prepared. During the construction of the schedule we looked at files in three of the local authorities in order to check what material was regularly available. As a result we omitted information which was not generally on file, such as details of the parents' employment and income. We were also alerted to the phenomenon of multiple home on trial placements; that is, different home on trial placements following directly on one from another as well as home on trial placements separated by a period in care or custody. We were able to design the schedule to accommodate these patterns.

The final schedule provided for the collection of over 200 items of information about the children and their families, as well as about some of the processes and practices that were involved in making and sustaining the placements. We also included three items on our subjective view of the standard of recording; one on the social work provided, and three on our judgement of the experience of the home on trial for the child. The last item was used as the basis for our evaluation.

We omitted from the sample of children home on trial those who were on remand or subject to interim care orders. For each local authority we divided the remaining children into groups according to their legal status. One group was composed of children on court orders for their protection made in care, divorce and wardship proceedings and also children who were subject to parental rights resolutions but allowed to be at home or with relatives. The other groups were children on orders for offending; for poor school attendance, and care orders that had resulted from the variation of supervision orders. From each of these groups we drew a one in three random sample except in the largest local authority where we took one in five. These procedures gave us similar numbers of children in each local authority and 321 children in all. Of these children, 20 had a sister or brother (or sometimes a half-sibling) in the study, but there are no sibling groups larger than two in the sample. Thus, our 321 children came from 301 families.

The limitation of this design is that since placements had been made at various times prior to 31st March, 1984, by this date they had already lasted for differing periods as table 1 makes clear. As far as the duration of the placements is concerned therefore, we are not comparing like with like. On the positive side this enabled us to gain a picture of the periods over which home on trial placements could extend. However, it may mean that long-term placements are somewhat over-represented and brief placements under-represented.

Table 1. Dates on which the Study Home on Trial Placement Started

	%
1972–79	10
1980–81	17
1982–83	60
1984	13
	——
	100
	——
	N = 321

The table above shows that the sample of children home on trial at the end of March, 1984 contained a majority who had started that placement less than two years before. However, for about a quarter, the placement had already lasted for more than two years.

We checked the distribution of the legal status of children in our sample against the distribution for England as a whole in 1984 and found that the percentage in every category but one was very similar That exception was children whose orders were varied from supervision orders to care orders under section 15(1) of the Children and Young Persons Act, 1969. Nationally only 4 per cent of children on such orders were home on trial in 1984 but in our sample this proportion was 21 per cent When working on the files we discovered that the legal status of children who had been on supervision orders, which were subsequently varied to care orders, was frequently recorded according to the section under which the care order was made, rather than as care orders under section 15(1). For example, a supervision order which was varied to a care order as a result of offending was often recorded as a section 7(7) order. In our sample we classified these children as section 15(1) cases although the local authorities had them coded otherwise in their DHSS returns. Thus, for example, one local authority had recorded only 14 children home on trial on 31st March, 1984 as being on care orders under section 15(1) or 7 per cent of its children home on trial. However, as a result of our correction we found that as many as 24 per cent of our sample in that local authority then fell into the section 15(1) category. The majority of 15(1) orders were used, we found, for offending and school attendance problems. The upshot of these errors in classification is that the annual returns made to the Department of Health substantially under-report the incidence of supervision orders being converted to care orders.[1]

It also emerged that some situations which were not strictly home on trial were recorded as if they were. During our exploratory stage, for example, we had already found cases such as a girl living in a flat with her baby, and a teenager missing for a year coded as home on trial. Other incorrect classifications offered to us by one local authority (though not necessarily on its returns to the DHSS) were cases of children in voluntary care under section II of the Child Care Act, 1980 and children fostered by relatives.[2] It is equally possible that some children who were technically home on trial were not classified as such by the local authorities. One particularly ambiguous situation was that of a young person who goes to live with a partner. The local authority, perhaps in the person of a clerical officer, then had the task of deciding whether such an arrangement was most suitably classified under the home on trial category or as 'in lodgings or living independently'.

In recording information from the case files we took the start of the care period as the date on which the full care order was made. Many children had been subject to interim care orders and some had been removed on a place of safety order prior to that. Wherever this occurred we noted it. However, the situation was more difficult in relation to parental rights resolutions under section III of the Child Care Act, 1980. A parental rights resolution could be applied for at any stage after a child had been received into care. We therefore decided, in the interests of comparability, to date the beginning of the care period for these children from the start of the last continuous period of voluntary care during which the parental rights resolution was taken.

Occasionally we found a home on trial placement that was sustained by the planned use of respite placements 'in care'. Where these were for periods not exceeding four weeks we did not record them as breaks in the home on trial placement. Termination of a home on trial placement was considered to have taken place if a child moved to a situation in which none of the original home on trial carers were present. Thus, if a child was placed with his mother and her cohabitee and the cohabitee subsequently left, the placement was deemed to continue. However, if the child then moved to live in the father's separate household the first home on trial placement was considered to have ended and a second home on trial placement to have begun. We discovered that the latter situation arose quite frequently as young people moved among relatives and friends without returning 'to care'.

It needs to be emphasised that the findings of the case file study relate solely to information recorded on file. Not all events will be noted and the information that is set down will necessarily be selective. It is unlikely to reflect fully or accurately the views of parents and children or of other participants. It also leaves out an account of the detailed services provided by staff in residential establishments, some of whom undertake considerable work towards rehabilitation and later the support of home on trial placements. Unfortunately this information was not routinely recorded on field work files.

We found that the files contained a wealth of information but that its extraction was very time-consuming. It was easier to work with the better organised files, particularly those that were arranged in sections. The hardest were those in one local authority which used 'family files' in which the information relating to all the children and some information on the parents was kept on one—or usually over time—a series of files. However, in all cases a crucial source of information for our purposes was the movement form kept on file, or the list of a child's movements stored at the beginning. Piecing together a child's history was extremely difficult if these were missing. The other crucial sources of information were court reports, six-monthly reviews, and reports of case conferences or residential reviews. In general, the forms used did not require social workers to give the reasons why the child went home on trial and, as a result, this information was not clearly available for 44 per cent of the children. For these cases, reasons had to be deduced from all the available information. Details of household composition were rarely required on review forms and were therefore rarely given. However, this could usually be found on the court reports (where, on the contrary, it is required) and from subsequent case notes. Even so, changes in household composition whilst the child was home on trial were hard to discover.

Six-monthly reviews were variable in quality and we considered that in about two-fifths of the cases they failed to provide a clear and full picture of the child's progress and development. In six-monthly reviews social workers tended to concentrate on the relationship of the child and the main home on trial carer. There was little information about the child's relationships with other children or with other adults in the household—a subject that our findings suggest is important. It was usually not clear who had been present at the six-monthly reviews, although it was generally expected that a senior member within the social services department would countersign the record. In one local authority the designation of the signatory was unspecified. When team leaders, and occasionally area directors, took an active part in supervising six-monthly reviews their written comments were sometimes very helpful and seemed to promote the active planning and management of the case.

Court reports usually presented a fairly good discussion of relevant issues past and present. Transfer summaries, when used, sometimes also did this but they were not as comprehensive or as sharply focused. Records of residential reviews were variable and were often presented in brief summary form, but sometimes they provided a good opportunity to discover the main events and plans that had been made. However, they often omitted information on the designation of participants. This was sometimes also true of case conferences. Undated documents, when they occurred, caused difficulties. There were also occasions when reference was made in the case notes to a case conference or review which could not be found on file.

In only one local authority was the level of authorisation for home on trial routinely recorded since a special form was used for this purpose. In the others it was necessary to work back to check the designation of signatories to the relevant six-monthly reviews, case conferences or residential reviews. Occasionally information about authorisation appeared in the case notes but agreement could have been given by a team leader or area director without it being recorded. The new regulations will clarify these matters for they require that the Director of Social Services, or a senior nominee, makes the decision on charge and control placements.

During the period of data collection, that is in 1986 and 1987, we held meetings with senior managers in the local authorities to discuss current policy and practice issues relating to home on trial.[3] At that time there were few written policies about home on trial placements or about the discharge of care orders in relation to specific requirements, such as the frequency of visiting or how quickly orders should be discharged. However, there were often general statements about child care policy and principles and they usually included a section on rehabilitation. These varied in their level of specificity. One document stated simply that 'where a child's removal from home is absolutely necessary this should be for the shortest possible time which it takes to rehabilitate him or her with his or her natural family or in his or her customary home'. Another document containing the child care policy for the local authority urged that for every admission to care there should be 'an initial plan of the purpose of the reception, how long the child is expected to remain in care, what is hoped to be achieved during that time and an initial statement of the necessary preconditions for rehabilitation'.

Had such principles routinely been translated into practice it would have led to greater clarity in the work undertaken while children were in care. This particular document continued with further statements concerning: the making of joint decisions between staff, parents and the child about what needed to be done, and by whom, in order to effect rehabilitation; the need to spell out the implications of failure; the need to hold regular reviews of progress; and the desirability of parents being involved in carrying out parental tasks for the child. Finally, it was stated that rehabilitation should take place within an agreed time that related to the age of the child, and that plans should be incorporated in a signed agreement. An annex by the NSPCC at the end of the document challenged the requirement that children should only be separated from parents if rehabilitation had been tried and failed. It was pointed out that in some cases of high risk rehabilitation should not be attempted.

The guidelines to practice produced by the third local authority contained a detailed statement about rehabilitation. As with the others, restoration was seen as a priority for children; a short time scale was urged and the need for the vigorous pursuit of the return of children to their families. Attention was directed to the importance of the choice of a placement that would promote work with the parents towards rehabilitation and access for parents was seen as crucial. There was also mention of the importance of a full assessment at the outset to determine whether rehabilitation should be pursued and a refreshing reference was made to the need to distinguish 'between what can and cannot be changed within a family' as well as to the possibility that assessment could indicate that rehabilitation was not feasible. It was suggested that the rehabilitation plan should address in detail the desired changes; how they were to be recognised; who would do what; and the time scale to be followed. The involvement of other agencies was also seen as important, as was sending written confirmation of the plan to all the parties and ensuring that the progress of the plan was reviewed regularly.

However, none of these documents referred to the legal status of children for whom rehabilitation was to be arranged. It may be because of this that no mention was made of the work needed to maintain children with their families once they had been returned to them, whether this had been by discharging children from care or placing them home on trial. Nor was there any reference to the responsibility carried by the local authority for children who were home on trial or any recommendations as to how that responsibility should be discharged.

However, whilst such statements embodied sound principles, they were rarely produced as a set of procedures for social workers to follow. As one team leader put it: 'the trouble is people dictate all sorts of things these days and one wonders if that's actual policy'. As a result, it appeared that in practice there was an absence of specific procedures relating to home on trial and that in fact social workers did not specify a time by which rehabilitation should be accomplished or an order discharged. There was no evidence of any specific requirements in relation to the use of written agreements, the involvement of parents and children in conferences and reviews, or in relation to the frequency with which social workers should visit during home on trial placements. Such omissions have, of course, now been made good by regulations that will bind all authorities in the same way.

The second part of our study involved interviews with social workers and parents who had current or recent experience of a home on trial placement. Since, of necessity, the number had to be small the exercise could not be representative. Therefore, we undertook the interviewing in only one of the local authorities. We selected two area offices and worked to a list of children who had been committed to care because of abuse, neglect or the incapacity of the parents but who were home on trial on 31st March, 1987. The interviews took place at the end of 1987. Interviews were held with six families where there was a child who had been or was still placed home on trial and with the social workers involved.

The interviews provided us with information about the experiences and views of parents and social workers who had first hand knowledge of home on trial placements and about the processes that led to the placements being made and the social work offered. It was unfortunate that severe limitations on our resources meant that we were unable to carry out more interviews. As a result it has not been possible to explore the views of a cross-section of parents or the views of a representative group of social workers. Nonetheless, the interviews furnished some rich information and form the basis for chapter 19. The names and certain details of the families described there and in the main body of the report have been changed in order to preserve confidentiality.

Notes and references

1. It is possible that when a supervision order is running a local authority will commence fresh care proceedings and discharge the supervision order. The care order would not then be made under section 15(1). One local authority we spoke to has used this procedure since 1986 in cases where there are concerns about immediate harm to a child: this is because the local authority solicitors had been informed that it was not possible to get an interim care order (except for the purpose of the completion

of a *guardian ad litem* report) in proceedings under section 15(1). Such a procedure might not be entirely clear from case files, but is probably unlikely to have been invoked very often, especially in cases of offending and school attendance.

2. That is, children subject to a care order or parental rights resolution who were placed with relatives who were classed as foster parents and received boarding-out allowances. There is some evidence that authorities with high rates of boarding-out with relatives have fewer children classified as home on trial.

3. We requested information about policy and practice issues relating to 1984, although the documents we have analysed were sometimes more recent. Nonetheless, it should be borne in mind that something over a third of the children in our sample had been made the subjects of compulsory care prior to 1980. Thus, in some cases their care careers had been exposed to a good deal of change in child care policies and practices.

CHAPTER 3

The Protected and the Disaffected

As the study progressed and as the data were analysed it became evident that there were substantial and significant differences[1] between the characteristics and care careers of the younger children for whom compulsory care was intended to provide protection and the older children who were on orders made principally to control their behaviour. We have called the first group the Protected and the second the Disaffected. Our division of the sample into these two categories was in large part dictated by their legal status. Thus the children upon whom care orders had been made because they were being ill-treated or neglected or whose proper development was being avoidably prevented[2] were placed in the Protected group. So were most of those who were subject to matrimonial care orders, wardship and parental rights resolutions. On the other hand, all the children subject to orders for offending, for not attending school or for being beyond their parents' control were allocated to the Disaffected group. Those where the grounds for the order had been their moral danger were also put into this group unless the order was clearly made on the basis of their sexual abuse.[3]

As a result of this classification 172 (54%) of our sample of 321 formed the Protected group and 149 (46%) the Disaffected. The detailed composition of each group according to the grounds for their compulsory care is set out in tables 2 and 3.

Table 2. The Grounds for the Compulsory Care of Children Placed in the Protected Group

(N = 172 for the Protected group unless otherwise stated)

	%
Care Order, neglect or abuse	57
Parental Rights Resolution	17
Matrimonial Care Order	17
Wardship	3
Care Order, variation of a Supervision Order	3
Care Order, moral danger	3
	100

Table 3. The Grounds for the Compulsory Care of Children Placed in the Disaffected Group

(N = 149 for the Disaffected group unless otherwise stated)

	%
Care Order, variation of a supervision order	36
Care Order, offending	25
Care Order, non-attendance at school	22
Care Order, beyond parental control	9
Care Order, moral danger	2
Matrimonial Care Order, Parental Rights Resolution	6
	100

The two groups were distinguished not only by the grounds for the orders but by the routes that the children had taken into compulsory care. Nearly half (49%) the Protected children had been subject to summary removal under a place of safety order, and half of these orders had been granted in respect of children under 5 years of age. Indeed, if we look only at Protected children on orders made under the Children and Young Persons Act, 1969 we find that three-quarters of these orders had been preceded by a place of safety order. In contrast, only 14 per cent of the Disaffected group of children had been removed on a place of safety order.[4] For nearly three-fifths of the Protected children the main ground for compulsory care was their abuse or neglect, or that of a sibling. For the remainder the initial ground was that their parents had been unable to look after them or that their care was jeopardised by marital struggles or poor housing conditions. In addition to the main grounds however there were often other concerns about these children when the order was made. For example, neglect was an additional concern for a quarter of them.

If precipitate removal characterised the route into care of the Protected children, the opposite was true for the Disaffected group, a considerable number of whom experienced a more gradual transition to compulsory care. Thirty-six per cent of the latter group had been on a supervision order which, because it was deemed unsuccessful, was then converted to a care order under section 15(1) of the Children and Young Persons Act, 1969. In contrast, section 15(1) orders were rarely used with the Protected children (only 3%). When the grounds for the variation of supervision orders were separated out, nearly half (45%) of the children in the Disaffected group were found to be on care orders where the main ground was offending and over a third (36%) where it was poor school attendance. One in five had been beyond the control of their parents or were considered to be in moral danger. Again, however, there were often additional concerns; for example, apart from where it was the main ground about a quarter of these young people were also considered to be beyond control and another quarter were poor school attenders.

There were other differences between our two groups. For example, whereas over half of the Protected group (56%) had spent time in care on a previous occasion, this only applied to about a third (31%) of the Disaffected.[5] Likewise, whereas in the Protected group boys and girls appeared in about equal number, boys outnumbered girls in the Disaffected group by 7 to 3. This is to be expected in a group comprising a large number of young offenders; but more boys than girls also appeared amongst the poor school attenders and amongst those regarded as being beyond their parents' control. By contrast all the children in the Disaffected group whose orders had been made on the grounds of their moral danger were girls: presumably the sexual activities of boys are not usually considered to warrant control by the community.[6]

The biggest difference between the Protected and the Disaffected groups was in their ages. In the Protected group 90 per cent were under 11 when they were committed to care,[7] whereas 88 per cent of the Disaffected group were older than this. Just over half of the Protected group were under 5 when they were made subject to compulsory care, whereas the age at which Disaffected children were most likely to be committed to care fell between their thirteenth and fifteenth birthdays. The tables below give this break-down.

Table 4. The Age of Children in the Protected Group at the Start of the Period of Compulsory Care in which the Home on Trial Placement in the Study Fell

	%
Less than 5 years	51
5–10 years	39
11 years +	10
	100

Table 5. The Age of Children in the Disaffected Group at the Start of the Period of Compulsory Care in which the Home on Trial Placement in the Study Fell

	%
5–10 years	12
11–12 years	24
13–14 years	45
15 years +	19
	100

The children's ages when placed home on trial reflected a similar pattern. Thus 78 per cent of the Protected group were under 13 when they went home on trial, whilst 91 per cent of the Disaffected were aged 13 or over. A more detailed breakdown of ages shows that over a quarter of the Protected children (27%) went home on trial under the age of 5, and two-fifths (38%) between the ages of 5 and 10. Among the Disaffected children the largest group went home on trial at the age of 16 or over (38%). Tables 6 and 7 summarise this information.

Table 6. Protected Group: Children's Age at which the Home on Trial Placement in the Study Started

	%
Less than 5 years	27
5–10 years	38
11 years	35
	100

Table 7. Disaffected Group: Children's Age at which the Home on Trial Placement in the Study Started

	%
5–10 years	4
11–12 years	5
13–14 years	29
15 years	24
16 years +	38
	100

The composition of the families from which the children in each group were removed was slightly but not significantly different. However, by the time they went home on trial significant differences between the family composition of the two groups emerged. Only a small proportion of Protected children went home on trial to both parents—just 17 per cent. This compared with 31 per cent for the Disaffected group. On the other hand, 40 per cent of the Protected children went to a step-parent (or parent plus partner) household, whereas only 18 per cent of the Disaffected children did so. Thus, the households of the Protected children frequently fragmented and re-formed in their absence: few children returned to both parents and many went to a reconstituted family or to a single parent. Indeed, 31 per cent of the Protected children returned to find that their parent's partner had changed in their absence, whilst this only occurred for 14 per cent of the Disaffected group. The families of Disaffected children were subject to much less change and significantly more of them went home on trial to both birth parents. Only a small proportion of children in both groups went home on trial at this stage to relatives. These details are shown in table 8.

Table 8. Family Composition at the Start of the Study Home on Trial (Adults only)

	Protected Group %	Disaffected Group %
Both parents	17	31
One parent	38	45
Parent and partner	40	18
Relatives	5	6
	100	100

Two-thirds (67%) of the Protected children were committed to care in the company of their siblings. (This included a quarter who were committed with one sibling and two-fifths committed with between two and five). The responsible social workers were thus often faced with the task of arranging accommodation for groups of brothers and sisters. In contrast, only a fifth (22%) of the Disaffected children were committed to care with their siblings and most of them with only one.[8] The pattern for these children was more often that care orders were made sequentially on each child in the family as they grew older and got into trouble.

At the stage of being placed home on trial, over two fifths (44%) of the Protected children returned with a sibling, whilst only 7 per cent of the Disaffected group did so. Ten per cent of both groups joined a sibling who was already home on trial when they returned. This is an underestimate of the frequency with which care orders had been made on the siblings of Disaffected children, since some of their older brothers and sisters who had been home on trial were instead in custody at the time that the child returned and others had been home on trial until the care order expired when they reached the age of 18. Indeed, over a third of the Disaffected children (36%) had brothers or sisters aged over 18 living at home when they went home on trial. This was true for only 6 per cent of Protected children. There were adult relatives and non-relatives living in two-fifths (41%) of the families to which the Disaffected children returned, but in only a fifth (18%) of Protected children's households.

Thus, significant differences existed between our two groups on a number of important dimensions. Indeed, we considered these to be so marked as to warrant treating the two groups separately in our description of the results. In part II we deal with the Protected group and in part III with the Disaffected.

However, before we leave this account of the contrasts between the two groups it is important to note that there were a number of factors which did not significantly differentiate between them. Two in particular might be mentioned. First, the composition (in terms of the principal carers) of the families from which the children were removed was not substantially different, although in both groups few had enjoyed an intact birth family by comparison with the general population.

Secondly, the ethnic composition of the two groups was not significantly different, although a somewhat larger proportion (20%) of the Protected group was black than of the Disaffected group (13%). Further analysis suggested certain differences *within* the black group, although numbers begin to be too small to draw firm conclusions. For example, whereas children of mixed parenthood were found in equal proportions in both groups, this was not the case for Afro-Caribbean and Asian children, nearly three-quarters of whom were in the protected group. This might be because care orders are less often used to control the behaviour of Afro-Caribbean and Asian adolescents than they are with other young people. Certainly a number of studies have commented on the over-representation of black teenagers in custody.[9] In their national study of child care placements Rowe and her colleagues found that taking both groups together, slightly fewer black children went home on trial than white children since fewer black children were on care orders.[10] Over and above these considerations, however, it is notable that we found little evidence in either of our groups of any significant differences between black and white children in the circumstances and outcomes of their placements home on trial.

Before concluding this chapter it is essential to re-emphasise that there are two distinct categories of children who, hitherto, have been classed together as being 'home on trial'. We have termed them the Protected and the Disaffected. That is not to deny that other differences exist amongst children who are home on trial and between their placements: plainly, they do, as we shall see. Nonetheless, the differences between the profiles of the Protected and the Disaffected groups are so pronounced that they must come to be acknowledged in both policy and practice.

Notes and references

1. In the account of our findings which follows in this chapter and in parts II and III, it should be noted that when statistically significant differences are reported, these are based upon the results in a chi-square test; that is, when $P < 0.05$.
2. See sections 1(2)a and b of the Children and Young Persons Act, 1969.
3. Of course, some of the adolescent girls whose behaviour was considered to put them in 'moral danger', might also have been subject to sexual abuse. However, we were attempting to categorise in terms of the issues on which the court had adjudicated.
4. See J. Packman, *Who Needs Care? Social Work Decisions About Children*, Blackwell, 1986. This study found that 34 per cent of all compulsory admissions were preceded by a place of safety order initiated by the social services department, with an additional 26 per cent initiated by the police. This compares with a total of 33 per cent for our whole sample. Some at least of the police place of safety orders in Packman's study reflected the dubious practice of taking place of safety orders on children for offending and truancy, which are not legal grounds for such orders.

5. This does not include time spent on place of safety orders and interim care orders immediately prior to full committal.

6. P. Cawson, 'The Sexist Social Worker? Some Gender Issues in Social Work Practice with Adolescent Girls', *Practice*, 1987. The author explores the sexist practices which lead to different dispositions being made for boys and girls for similar acts. Authorities tend to equate sexual freedom in girls with law breaking. For boys their sexuality is only the subject of concern if homosexuality is involved.

7. This is the age at which the court order was made, not including place of safety orders and interim care orders. However, for children on parental rights resolutions, this is their age at the start of the last continuous period of voluntary care during which the resolution was made.

8. See S. Millham, R. Bullock, K. Hosie and M. Haak, *Lost in Care: the Problems of Maintaining Links between Children in Care and their Families*, Gower, 1986. Nearly half the children in their sample entered care with one or more siblings, but their sample, unlike ours, included children in voluntary care. The proportion for our whole sample was 46 per cent.

9. See for example, J. Tipler, *Juvenile Justice in Hackney*, Hackney Social Services Department, 1986, and National Association for the Care and Resettlement of Offenders, *Grave Crimes, Grave Doubts*, 1988.

10. J. Rowe, M. Hundleby and L. Garnett, *Child Care Now: A Survey of Placement Patterns*, British Agencies for Adoption and Fostering, 1989.

CHAPTER 4

Evaluation

So little has been known about home on trial placements that a purely descriptive study would have made a considerable contribution. However, social workers who have to decide whether or not a child who is committed to care should be allowed home need as much guidance from research as possible. Such assistance could only be provided if the information that we collected was related to an evaluation of the placements. We have endeavoured to do this although there are, of course, difficulties to be faced. We return to consider some of these later, but in this chapter we explain how we evaluated the placements and with what results.

After reading each file carefully we assessed whether, in our judgement, the placement had been positive for the child; adequate; unsatisfactory or detrimental. In coming to our conclusions we maintained a firm focus upon the child and his or her experience rather than that of the parents, carers or the departments. Furthermore, we did not automatically class a placement as unsatisfactory or detrimental if a child re-offended, was troublesome in the community or failed to attend school regularly. Nonetheless, we strove to place the child's experiences at home within as full a developmental context as possible. Few placements are positive on all counts and few completely negative. There are off-setting considerations which present a complicated equation to anyone devising a means of evaluation, not least the question of how much better or worse some other arrangement might have been. After much consideration and a number of trial runs with other approaches to these problems we decided that we should record systematically our own judgement of each placement after undertaking a thorough review of all the information on file.

In adopting this approach we obviously expose ourselves to a number of criticisms: it is somewhat unusual for researchers to build their judgements into the evaluative design of a project. However, we would defend our decision to do so on several grounds. First, since we had discussed and agreed the yardsticks of our assessments and undertook the extraction of data from the files ourselves, we had a good chance of reaching a reasonable degree of standardisation in our judgements, leaving aside for the moment the issue of whether they were well-founded. Secondly, of necessity we had to become immersed in each of the files, spending hours in assembling and ferreting out information. We felt that our familiarity with the record was as great as it could be and therefore that we were justified in drawing conclusions on the basis of that evidence. We suspect that few social workers have the opportunity and time to read their files so thoroughly, especially those that cover long periods. Thirdly, we were not unfamiliar with the practice of social work or with the problems faced in these matters by departments, carers and children alike.

Finally, we did endeavour to test our judgements against those of other people who occupied a variety of roles in and around child care. We took twenty of the cases that we considered presented difficult issues of evaluation and, working from our field notes and the collected data, we compiled a fairly brief account of the placement and what had happened. We then asked our selected group to judge these placements employing the same criterion (that is, benefit or detriment to the child) that we had used. The group included social workers, middle managers in social services departments, a psychiatrist, a senior social work teacher, a number of members of the National Association of Young People in Care, some parents of children in care (with whom the Family Rights Group had put us in contact) and a grandparent of a child in care who belonged to the Grandparents' Federation.

In 12 out of the 20 selected cases 10 or more of the 'panel' of 15 were in agreement about whether or not the placement had been positive or negative on a simple two-option question. Our assessments were in line with the majority in all these instances. They were also the same in five out of the eight remaining cases where there was only a small majority one way or the other.

We felt reassured by this exercise, at least to the extent that our judgements were only at odds with a majority of the panel in three cases where there was in any case a narrow 8 to 7 split. In all there were five cases upon which the panel were so divided.

The replies of those involved only suggested one cluster of responses. The three social work managers were markedly more positive in their assessments than the others. When we compared our assessments with those of the panel on a fourfold rather than a twofold classification, we found that we had tended somewhat in this direction as well.

The other fact that encouraged us deliberately to include our own judgements in the design was the difficulty of devising an alternative method that did not fall prey to other shortcomings. All methods of making evaluations have been subjected to telling criticisms, usually along the lines that they distort by treating complicated situations too simply. For example, when social workers are asked to evaluate the outcomes of their own cases the charge is that they are inclined to regard matters too favourably and to offer interpretations that are coloured by hindsight. On the other hand, when more 'objective' criteria are employed as a basis for evaluation (such as the duration of placements) research exposes itself to the criticism that it cannot be assumed that because one arrangement has survived longer than another it has been more satisfactory. Of course, it would be desirable to incorporate consumer evaluation (on the part of both children and parents) but the problems of actually organising such a study are considerable if the aim is to include a sufficiently large number of cases to enable a convincing analysis to be undertaken. Although, as we have explained, we did talk to parents who had experienced a home on trial placement, we did not do so in a systematic fashion.

The results of our evaluations for the Protected and the Disaffected groups respectively are set out in table 9.

Table 9. Evaluation of Placements: Research Judgements

	Protected Group		Disaffected Group		Total	
	No.	%	No.	%	No.	%
Positive	81	47	61	41	142	44
Adequate	51	30	60	40	111	35
Unsatisfactory	10	6	19	13	29	9
Detrimental	25	15	6	4	31	10
Not clear	5	3	3	2	8	2
	172	100	149	100	321	100

Two things need to be noted about these results. First, there were eight cases where we felt unable to make a judgement (usually for want of enough information) and, secondly, there was a significant difference between the

Protected and Disaffected groups. The placements of the Protected group were more likely to be judged as either positive or detrimental than those of the Disaffected group. These were more likely to have been allocated to the two intermediate groups. However, given the distribution in table 9 we decided that for most of the further analysis we would treat our evaluations as a simple dichotomy: 'positive' and 'negative' (including those that were not clear). However, in collapsing the categories in this way some of the difference between our two groups is obscured. It is important, therefore, to bear in mind that where the placements were not positive they were more likely to be clearly detrimental to those in the Protected group than they were for those amongst the Disaffected. In that sense it might be argued that the placements home of the Protected children ran greater risks than those of the Disaffected group.

Despite the advantages of our making evaluations in the way that has been described there are obvious drawbacks as well. With these in mind we also undertook a more traditional child care evaluation based upon whether the placements survived or broke down during our two-year follow-up. The results of this method of evaluation are set out in table 10.

Table 10. Evaluation of Placements According to Whether they Broke Down or Not in the Follow-up Period

	Protected Group		Disaffected Group		Total	
	No.	%	No.	%	No.	%
Did not break down	104	62	75	50	185	57
Broke down	63	38	74	50	136	43
	*167	100	149	100	321	100

(*Information was not sufficiently clear to classify five cases)

Employing this rather more conventional evaluation it will be seen that there was a somewhat higher overall 'success' rate of 57 per cent; but that there was also a statistically significant difference between the placements of the Protected and the Disaffected groups, with the Protected cases being less likely to break down than the Disaffected category. It is, however, interesting to compare the results of our two methods of evaluating the home on trial placements in more detail. Table 11 shows how many cases were similarly and differently classified by the two systems.

Table 11. Comparison of the Evaluations made by Research Judgement and by Whether or Not the Placements Broke Down

	Protected Group		Disaffected Group		Total	
	No.	%	No.	%	No.	%
Identically classified	117	70	103	69	220	70
Differently classified	50	30	46	31	96	30
	*167	100	149	100	316	100

(*Information was not sufficiently clear to classify five cases)

As can be seen, there is no difference between the rates of identical classification (whether positive or negative) between the two groups. However, in both categories the differences in classification as between the two methods of evaluation arose both from our classing as 'negative' some placements that continued and from our classing some of those that terminated as 'positive'.

The fact that compared with our panel's assessments our judgements veered towards the positive side whilst when they were compared with assessments based upon whether placements survived or broke down they veered towards the negative, provided further reassurance that in using 'researcher judgements' as the basis for evaluation we were not obtaining what might be regarded as 'extreme' results. It is these evaluations that we employ in presenting the main body of our findings in parts II and III.

PART II

The Protected Children
Home on Trial

CHAPTER 5

Turmoil and Risk

Turmoil

Our Protected group comprised 172 children, girls and boys in almost equal number. When they went home on trial 27 per cent were under 5 and 65 per cent under 10. One in five of them were black (including those of mixed parentage). Seventeen per cent were subject to a parental rights resolution and the same proportion to a matrimonial care order. The majority of the group had been neglected or physically abused, and 12 had suffered sexual abuse. More than half (56%) had been in care before the occasion that led to the home on trial placement, and almost the same proportion had experienced more than one placement during their current episode in care; indeed, a quarter had had four or more.

Thus the children were mainly young and many had suffered harm at the hands of their parents or their parent's partners. They came from disrupted and volatile households; only 28 per cent had been living with both birth parents immediately prior to their committal. Although 45 per cent came into care from one-parent households that proportion is misleading since between the time that the events precipitating the order occurred and the order was made some partners had left. For example, 19 (11%) of the children in this Protected group were not removed from home, either because an abusing adult had departed or, in the case of certain matrimonial care orders and wardship cases, because committal to care was being used to confirm or reinforce the custody of a particular parent.[1] As might be expected, placements where children were not removed from home

[35]

(although committed to care) were significantly related to successful outcomes.

The decision to allow children home, therefore, was by no means straightforward or risk-free. Unfortunately, some of the terminology encourages a simplification of what are in fact complicated situations. Take, for example, the idea of returning 'home'. We have seen already that whilst the children were away in care their families had not stood still. When they went home on trial nearly a third of them (31%) found that their parent's partner had left or been replaced, or that the relationship that they had had with a single parent now had to be shared with a new cohabitee or step-parent. Other children had to make other adjustments since about one in six of them (16%) did not go home on trial to the household which they had left but to one that was entirely different. For most of them this involved going to the other parent (for example, after having been removed from the mother's household they went home on trial to the father's) and a few went home on trial to relatives or, occasionally, the move was from a relative's household to be home on trial with a parent. Put together it can be seen that just under half of the Protected group of children went home on trial either to a completely different household or to one in which there had been changes in their parent's partnership. Thus, many of these placements involved entry to a new household rather than a return to the one that had been left. The pattern can be seen in table 12.

Table 12. Changes in the Composition of the Household (Main Carers only) to which the Child went Home on Trial

	%
Never removed from home	11
No change	42
Parent's partner had changed	31
Different parent/carer(s)	16
	——
	100
	——

Yet these were not the only changes that returning children had to face. Often brothers, sisters and step-siblings had arrived on the scene or had departed. Other adults or grown-up siblings came and went. Over half of the children (58%) found that such changes had occurred in their absence. Many had to contend with a combination of changes. Taking all changes together (that is to parents, children and other adults), three-quarters of the children were affected: only a quarter found the household that they had left unchanged on their return.[2] This is an important fact that does not always seem to be fully appreciated: it has considerable implications for social workers preparing for and managing home on trial.

Risk

These various findings underline the complicated nature of the placements. Other results give evidence of the risks. For example, 42 children were abused or neglected in some way whilst they were home on trial; this is a quarter of all the Protected children. Twenty children were abused physically and two sexually. The other 20 suffered marked neglect in terms of very poor physical care or periods of being left alone without supervision.

Of the 22 children who were abused whilst home on trial, nine had originally been committed on grounds other than abuse. Similarly, whilst 20 children were neglected during home on trial, for six of them the concerns which had brought them into compulsory care had not revolved around neglect. Thus, although the grounds for compulsory care were an indication of risks during home on trial, it is important to note that they were not the whole story. In particular, the risks of abuse and neglect were quite closely linked. A number of children who had been committed to care because of abuse went on to suffer neglect during home on trial, and some whose entry to care was on the grounds of neglect were subsequently abused.

None of the 12 children who were originally committed to care as a result of being sexually abused were reported to have been sexually abused during home on trial. Even so, as we have seen, there were two children who were committed on other grounds who were.

Of course, it is likely that considerable caution was exercised in returning sexually abused children home on trial, and in most cases the perpetrator was no longer in the household. However, the situation was rather different in the cases of physical abuse, where two-thirds of the children were returned to at least one of the parents who had abused them. A higher proportion (25%) of these children were re-abused whilst home on trial than children who were returned to a household in which the abusing parent was no longer present (10%). Nonetheless, as can be seen, the absence of the original abuser is not necessarily a guarantee of the subsequent safety of the child.

The complicated nature of the risks involved in return is further illustrated by the fact that 17 per cent of the children who had been committed to care because a brother or a sister had been abused were themselves subjected to abuse during home on trial. This compared with a re-abuse rate of 26 per cent for the children who had been the subjects of the original abuse. The previously unabused siblings of an abused child were not immune from risk when they went home.

Thus a quarter of the children suffered abuse or neglect of varying levels of seriousness whilst they were home on trial (42 children). However, most of them stayed in the home on trial placement. Only nine were removed as the direct result of their abuse or neglect. For another three children where the placement ended mainly for other reasons, the abuse or neglect of the child also played a part. The rest remained in the home on trial placement or subsequently left for other reasons. Incidents of abuse and neglect during home on trial were dealt with in a number of ways, but in only a minority of cases did such an incident lead directly to the child's removal. We return later to the important issues that this finding raises.

The concept of 'risk' does not only involve abuse or neglect, although these are the easier dimensions with which to grapple. A substantial minority of children (one in seven) had serious behaviour problems at home or school, or often both, whilst they were home on trial. Furthermore, attendance at school or day nursery was poor or non-existent for a fifth of them (21%). There was also some offending: among those who were over ten by the end of the placement, 20 per cent had offended at least once. Of 37 teenage girls, five (14%) became pregnant during home on trial. However, as we shall see later, rates of poor school attendance, offending and pregnancy among adolescent members of the Protected group were on a very much lower scale than they were amongst those in the Disaffected group.

There were fairly high levels of concern about the situation of Protected children once they were living at home on trial. Schools, day nurseries and neighbours reported anxieties about the health or welfare of over a quarter of them (27%). Children who were subjected to abuse and neglect during home on trial were far more frequently the focus of such reports than other children. Similarly, few of the home on trials which we evaluated as positive had raised concern in the local community, whereas nearly two-thirds of the placements which we judged to have been detrimental had done so. This suggests that when such reports are received they should be taken seriously. It was our impression that opinions that differed from the prevailing view of the social services departments (particularly those from schools) were sometimes put on one side and, for example, not mentioned in the main body of the six-monthly reviews for which they had been written.

It is tempting to believe that risks and difficulties subside as time passes, and this was certainly true in some cases. On the other hand, when placements broke down or crises arose they often did so after the child had been 'home' for quite a long time. Given that home on trial placements are generally thought to be a prelude to the discharge of orders if all goes well it was surprising to find how long many of these trial periods had lasted. Two-fifths (39%) of the home on trial placements had continued for three years or more and the average was just over three years. The shortest placement had survived for only a month whilst the longest had been going on for twelve and a half years.

Looked at somewhat differently we found that of the 63 (38%) placements that broke down only a little over a quarter did so within the first year, whilst well over a third happened after more than two years. The general message of these findings is that risks and problems are not peculiar to the early stages of a home on trial placement. The passage of time, of itself, is no indication that supervision can be relaxed; it is the context and the circumstances in which the prolongation of the placement occurs that have to be considered first.

*   *   *

Despite the obvious nature of many of the risks and difficulties associated with placing children home on trial it is of great importance to stress that we judged nearly half (47%) of the placements in the Protected group to have been positive for the child. It is crucial, therefore, to be able to say, as far as possible, what it is that distinguished the successful placements from those which were not. We have borne this firmly in mind in what follows. However, there are two distinct clusters of information that have to be taken into account. First, there is that information which could be known at the point when a decision to allow a child home on trial is being made. Secondly, there are the factors which only become apparent once the placement has been made. Some things cannot be known before the event.

If social workers and others are to be helped in deciding about and managing home on trial placements it is essential for these two groups of information to be differentiated. Current decisions can only draw upon knowledge of the past, albeit that that is employed to assess future likelihoods. Hence, in the next chapter we consider what had happened to the children and their families prior to the start of the home on trial. After that we look at what occurred as the placement unfolded.

Notes and references

1. The number of children not removed from home at the outset when committed to care was actually 26 (or 15%). However, seven of them were subsequently removed before being placed home on trial again. Unless otherwise stated we refer to the lower figure as the number (11%) not having been removed from home.

2. In our sample as a whole (both the Protected and Disaffected groups) we found that two-thirds of the children's families changed their structure while the child was away. This is a similar proportion to that found in Millham *et al., op. cit.* Such changes are not confined to children in compulsory care. Stevenson and Smith, for example, found that between 35 and 50 per cent of children leaving 'voluntary' care returned to families that were differently composed to those that they had left. (O. Stevenson and J. Smith, *Report of the Implementation of Section 56 of the Children Act, 1975,* Department of Social Policy and Social Work, University of Keele, 1983).

CHAPTER 6

The Children's Past Experiences

Disruption

We have already noted that many of the children in the sample had complicated care histories. It will be recalled that over half (56%) had been in care at least once before the committal to care which led to the placement at 'home'. Furthermore, during their current episode of care more than half of them (55%) had also experienced at least two placements, and a quarter four or more. Thus many of the Protected group of children had had to face an assortment of disruptions. Such a succession of upheavals could be expected to have made the transition back to their families especially difficult.

Our fears on this score were borne out, since we found that those who had had only one placement in care prior to returning home on trial were significantly more likely to do well than the children who had experienced more than one. It is of particular interest however that the rate of positive outcomes fell sharply even between one and two placements. Of course, selectivity may have been at work here with the more difficult children having to be transferred more often. Nonetheless, some placements end for reasons that are unconnected with children's behaviour; for example, as a result of the illness of foster parents or because of the closure of a community home. Even so, it was certainly our impression that children who were functioning fairly adequately at the start of their care careers could become increasingly disturbed with each successive change of placement. Other research bears this out: Lynch and Roberts[1] found that the abused children in their study who had 'lost' more than one family during their follow-up were likely to show overt behaviour disturbances. Hensey and his colleagues also found that the more placements that abused children had had the worse the outcome.[2]

Paradoxically, however, as we shall see, there was a group of children whose placement home on trial could be considered to have been the result of their disturbed behaviour. In cases where all else seemed to have failed, return home (especially for the somewhat older children) could be the reluctantly accepted option of last resort.

Numerous factors determine how many placements a child experiences as well as the relationship that this has to whether he or she goes home (and when) and to what happens afterwards. This complexity can be illustrated by the fact that successful outcomes were significantly associated with return home from foster homes rather than from residential establishments. Stepping beyond this finding however, it was evident that having been in a foster home prior to going home on trial was also significantly related to having had only one placement, and that of a relatively short duration. By contrast, the children who went home from residential care were more likely to have had multiple placements and to have been in care longer.

The length of time children had spent in care was important since we found that a positive experience during home on trial was significantly associated with short stays in care; that is, periods of less than a year. Hensey and his colleagues obtained similar results in their study[3] and Berridge and Cleaver found that long durations in care before a child was placed in a foster home foreshadowed subsequent breakdown.[4] Overall, a third of our Protected group had been in care for under a year; a third for one to three years, and another third for more than three years before they went home on trial.

Timing and Age

Of course, many of the children who are returned home quickly may have come from the families who were judged to have the least severe problems. However, that was not always the case. Plans for the early rehabilitation of a child were more likely to have been made for abused children than for those who had been neglected or who were subject to matrimonial care orders or parental rights resolutions. Even so, it would be unwise for social workers to assume from our results that the chances of a placement back home being successful will automatically improve as long as the decision is taken early in the child's care career; but if there are no contra-indications it certainly appears that the rule of 'the earlier the better' applies.

That is obviously related to the question of the child's age. As we have seen, the majority (78%) of the Protected group of children were under 13 when they went home on trial and over a quarter (27%) were under five. The mean age at placement was $8\frac{1}{2}$ years. Table 13 gives the details.

Table 13. The Age of Children when they were Placed Home on Trial

	%
Less than 2 years	9
2–4 years	18
5–7 years	18
8–10 years	20
11–12 years	13
13–14 years	13
15 years or more	9
	100

Many studies of fostering have shown that the child's age at placement is very important in terms of outcome.[5] Our work also showed the relevance of age in the case of placements home on trial. Children under the age of two did best, those aged two to seven the next best, followed by children of from eight to twelve. Those aged thirteen or over had the fewest successful outcomes.

Residential Homes and Foster Care

Let us return for a moment, however, to consider a potentially important result concerning the previous placements of children-going home on trial. Immediately prior to returning almost half (49%) had been living in residential homes and approaching two-fifths (37%) were in foster care. Table 14 gives the details.

Table 14. Placement Prior to Home on Trial

	%
Never removed from home	11
Foster Home	37
Residential care	49
Other	3
	100

It is interesting to note that of the foster placements from which protected children returned home on trial, 11 per cent were foster placements with relatives.[6] Most Protected children in residential care were in community homes but 13 per cent were in observation and assessment centres. Only one Protected child got home by absconding and no children went home on trial directly from hospital.

The type of placement from which children went home on trial was related to age. Sixty four per cent of the children who went home on trial under the age of five went from foster homes and a rather astonishing 36 per cent from residential care. However, for children aged five and over but less than eight the proportions were equally divided between residential and foster care, whilst for children aged eight to thirteen 70 per cent returned from residential care. Thus, even young children were in residential care prior to returning home. This is in part explained by the fact that a quarter of the Protected children were on care orders made between 1972 and 1980 when greater use was made of residential care, including residential nurseries. Nonetheless, even taking this into account, the high rates of residential care are surprising.[7]

Whereas half of the Protected children returned home from a residential placement, in England as a whole at the start of 1984 only 21 per cent of children on the kinds of orders included in our sample were in residential care. At the same time, whilst 37 per cent of the Protected children in the study went home on trial from a foster home, the equivalent proportion of children who were in foster care in England was 71 per cent.[8] It appears, therefore, that a disproportionately large group of children going home on trial came from residential care and that a smaller proportion than would be expected arrived from foster homes. This could have reflected a preference for residential care for children intended for speedy rehabilitation, as suggested in the Dartington study *Lost in Care*.[9] However, this did not appear to be the case since rehabilitation was planned at the outset for far more children who returned home on trial from a foster placement (43 per cent of those placements) than for children returning from residential care (only 25 per cent). Furthermore, of children who did return speedily (within six months) 69 per cent did so from a foster placement and only 31 per cent from residential care. It may be that some children whose foster placements have broken down end up in residential care and that either their difficult behaviour or their unsatisfactory care experiences are influential in getting them placed home on trial. Our figures show that only 17 children had moved from a former placement and then spent less than six months in the residential establishment from which they went home on trial. However, we do not know whether these earlier moves were from foster care or why they were made.

Nonetheless, an intriguing picture emerges. Even though, as we have seen, definite intentions for rehabilitation were far more often associated with foster placements than with residential care, and speedy returns home on trial were most often from foster homes, residential care remained a major feeder system for home on trial. A significantly disproportionately large group of children who returned home came from residential care. It would appear therefore that there are powerful factors that either inhibit children returning from foster care or which promote their return from residential establishments, or both.

One possibility is that children in residential establishments may be the recipients of regular visits from their families since, as Aldgate has shown, parents often find it easier to visit their children when they are in residential care than when they are in foster care, and telephone contact is often more possible with children in residential care.[10] Children may also make regular visits home at weekends as part of the routine of the establishment, especially when staff complements are low at weekends. Such patterns might well have been important since studies by both Aldgate and by Fanshel[11] have shown that there is a direct correlation between the amount of parental visiting and involvement and a child's eventual return home.

It may be, therefore, that the regular contact between child and family that was built into placements in some residential establishments both maintained the child's contact with home and in due course, led to return taking place. Indeed, among the Protected children in our study 92 per cent of those in residential care had been spending week-ends at home in the three months before returning home on trial. This compared with 65 per cent of the children in foster home placements. Very few children in residential care had no visits or weekends home, while this was the case for 14 per cent of the children who went home on trial from foster care.

At the same time other factors that are specific to residential care may play a part in encouraging a child's return home; for example, social workers' dissatisfaction with residential care as a long-term placement or the rehabilitation efforts made by residential staff. It may be that the regularity and scope of residential reviews also contribute to returns since, as Sinclair's study has shown, these tend to be more purposeful and to entertain a longer-term perspective than those held in area offices.[12] Certainly, as we shall see later, in our study a review meeting was held to discuss the home on trial placement for most of the children in residential care but for only a small proportion of the children in foster homes.

As Aldgate has shown, visits to children in foster homes may be uncomfortable for both parents and foster parents[13] and, as other studies have illustrated, social work activity to maintain visits may be insufficient or may decline over time.[14] In addition, there may be a greater reluctance to move children home from a settled foster placement than there is to move them from a residential establishment. This was shown by Vernon and Fruin who found that 'whilst in the period immediately following admission, the child's being in care was explained in terms of the parents, subsequent explanations increasingly focused on accounts of how settled the child had become in his or her foster home'.[15] Thus, it seems that the importance of residential care as a route to home on trial is a product of factors within residential care which promote return combined with factors within foster care which act in the opposite direction. This issue clearly needs to be kept in mind as more and more emphasis is placed both on the desirability of foster care and on children's rehabilitation with their families. The policies may not be entirely compatible without important adjustments in practice.

Re-trials

One of the results of our study that surprised us was the number of placements home on trial that the children had already had. Over a fifth (22%) of the Protected children in the sample had been placed home on trial on a previous occasion without success, usually with the same household. A few children already had two or three unsuccessful home on trial placements behind them. Having traced their histories and watched with sinking heart as some were returned yet again to fragile families, it was not surprising to find that children were more likely to have a home on trial which we evaluated as successful if they had not had a previous home on trial with the same carer. Again, Berridge and Cleaver found that foster placements did best when they were the first attempt. Previous failed foster placements were significantly associated with further breakdown.[16] The lesson seems to be that if home on trial has not worked on a previous occasion very careful thought needs to be given to trying it for the second time. The question that has to be answered is: what has changed that will make it work now when it did not do so before? This is certainly the view put forward by Maluccio and his colleagues.[17] The dangers of a 'try again' policy were also shown in the study of abused children by Lynch and Roberts.[18] They consider that if a rehabilitation breaks down, a definite decision is needed on the child's future care. In addition, we found that when a second home on trial placement was attempted, children did better if at least a year had elapsed between the two placements. This again suggests that the situation needs to have altered significantly before the child returns home on trial on a second occasion.

It is interesting to see what had caused these 37 earlier home on trial placements to end. We found that a third had ended because of family break-up (including illness or imprisonment of the carers) and the remainder because of neglect, abuse, a breakdown in relationship with the child, or for reasons associated with the child's behaviour.

*   *   *

Thus, a number of factors in a child's previous history discriminated between those placements home on trial which were likely to succeed and those which were not. In particular, the shorter the time that the child had been away the better; the less disrupted their care careers the better; and the younger they were the better. On the other hand second or third attempts at making the same home on trial placement were unlikely to be any more successful than the first. None of this is unexpected; but it does re-emphasise the need to minimise disruption for children in care and for an early start to be made on rehabilitation wherever it appears to be a reasonable possibility.

Notes and references

1. M.A. Lynch and J. Roberts, *The Consequences of Child Abuse*, Academic Press, 1982.
2. O.J. Hensey, J.K. Williams and L. Rosenbloom, 'Intervention in Child Abuse: Experience in Liverpool', in *Developmental Medicine and Child Neurology*, 25, 1983.
3. *Ibid.*
4. Berridge and Cleaver, *op. cit.*
5. For example, R.A. Parker, *Decision in Child Care*, Allen and Unwin, 1966; V. George, *Foster Care: Theory and Practice*, Routledge and Kegan Paul, 1970; Berridge and Cleaver, *op. cit.*, and G. Trasler, *In Place of Parents*, Routledge and Kegan Paul, 1960.
6. Our numbers were small but, by comparison, in England on 31.3.84, 13 per cent of foster placements were with relatives. *Children in Care of Local Authorities for the Year Ending 31 March, 1984, England*, DHSS, 1985.
7. Rowe *et al.* (1988), *op. cit.* Analysis of the 4940 admissions and subsequent placements of children in 1985 and 1986 showed that 5 per cent of children under 5 were placed in residential care and 25 per cent of those aged between 5 and 11.

8. *Children in Care of Local Authorities for the Year Ending 31 March, 1984, England*, DHSS, *op. cit.* Section III cases cannot be isolated from the DHSS statistics and therefore all such cases have had to be excluded from this calculation. It should also be noted that because of the way we drew our sample, children had been placed home on trial on varying dates up to and including 1984. Thus, some of the usage of residential placements could be accounted for by the fact that a quarter of the home on trial placements had been made prior to 1981. However, since the remainder were made from 1981 onwards, they do reflect fairly recent practice.

9. Millham *et al.* (1986), *op. cit.*

10. J. Aldgate, *The Identification of Factors Influencing Children's Length of Stay in Care*, Ph.D thesis, University of Edinburgh, 1977.

11. Aldgate (1977), *op. cit.*; D. Fanshel, 'Parental Visiting of Children in Foster Care: Key to Discharge?' in *Social Services Review*, vol. 49, no. 4, 1975; D. Fanshel, 'Status Changes of Children in Foster Care: Final Results of the Columbia University Longitudinal Study', in *Child Welfare*, vol. 55, no. 3, 1976.

12. R. Sinclair, *Decision Making in Statutory Reviews in Children in Care*, Gower, 1984.

13. Aldgate (1977), *op. cit.*

14. V. George, *op. cit.* This study showed the lack of active encouragement for parents to maintain contact with children in foster care. Millham *et al.* (1986), *op. cit.*, showed the marked decline in social work activity the longer the child was in care. Contact with parents dropped sharply. J. Vernon and D. Fruin, *In Care: A Study of Social Work Decision Making*, National Children's Bureau, 1986, showed that once a child was in care, priority shifted to more pressing cases.

15. Vernon and Fruin, *op. cit.*

16. Berridge and Cleaver, *op. cit.*

17. A.N. Maluccio, E. Fein and K.A. Olmstead, *Permanency Planning for Children: Concepts and Methods*, Tavistock, 1986.

18. Lynch and Roberts, *op. cit.*

CHAPTER 7

The Home in Prospect

The Restructuring of Households

We have already seen that when the children went 'home' they entered households which were often substantially different from the ones that they had left. Only a quarter returned to an identical household and 16 per cent were confronted with one which was entirely different.[1] Whereas 28 per cent of the children had been with both parents when the order was made, this proportion had dropped even further by the time they returned. Only 17 per cent of them went home on trial to both parents. At the same time, there were also fewer parents on their own: the previous proportion of 45 per cent had declined to 38 per cent. This was accounted for by an increase in the proportion of children going home on trial to one parent and a new partner—which by then represented 40 per cent of the home on trial placements (as opposed to 24 per cent when the orders were made). Clearly, the reconstitution of families was an important feature of many home on trial placements. The details are set out in table 15.

Table 15. Composition of Households (Main Carers only)

	Households from which Children Entered Care %	Households to which Children Returned %
Both parents	28	17
One parent	45	38
One parent and partner	24	40
Relatives	3	5
	100	100

[49]

The outcomes that were associated with these different household changes are of considerable interest. Placements with a father and step-mother or cohabitee appeared to be the most vulnerable. Although the numbers were relatively small the difference was statistically significant. The poor quality of such placements did not appear to be a result simply of difficulties associated with household reconstruction since placements with a mother and stepfather or cohabitee did better than those with a father and stepmother. Information from the case notes suggested that difficulties in these latter families often arose because although it was on the father's account that the child went to live in the family, it was expected that most of the care would be undertaken by the woman. This could put a strain on relationships, especially if the woman had children of her own, and mutual resentment could cause rejection of the returned child or the collapse of the marriage or cohabitation.

Children did best home on trial when there had been no change in the household to which they went or where there had *only* been a change in their parent's partner. Children did least well when there were changes amongst the *children* in the household. This would suggest that attention needs to be focused on the children in the new household as well as upon the adults; all the more so since the alteration in the membership of children in the household had an adverse effect even when there had not been a change among the adult carers. This indicates even more strongly the crucial importance of the child's relationships with siblings and step-siblings and their critical impact on the relationship with the parents; for example, through sibling rivalry and competition for the parents' time and affection. The birth of a baby in the family might arouse feelings of displacement and envy in the returning child, the resolution of which would depend upon many factors including the child's age and how the necessary re-adjustments were managed by the family. It was not apparent how social workers regarded the question of returning a child when a baby was imminent. Sometimes the child seemed to have been rushed home before the birth. In general it was unclear how the risk of return at a time of stress was balanced against the likely restructuring of relationships in the child's absence. However, it seems probable that the installation of stepchildren whilst the child was away might well pose problems—again depending upon the relative ages of the children and the overall pattern and quality of family relationships.

These results about children in the household echo many of those in studies of fostering. As long ago as the early 1960s, for example, Parker found that the probability of a placement failing was increased when foster parents had children of their own, especially if they were under five or of a similar age to the foster child.[2] George's study in 1970[3] and Berridge and Cleaver's much later work[4] largely confirmed these results.

It is interesting to note that only nine (5%) of the children went home on trial to relatives; eight to grandparents and one to a sibling. We judged seven to have been positive. However, as we shall see, home on trial placements with relatives grew in importance later as some children moved around the extended family.

The households to which the Protected children went tended to be large. Only a quarter (28%) entered a small household (2–3 members including the child) but a third (33%) went to households which contained six or more members including the child. Just under a quarter of the children (23%) were the only child in the family, whilst for 29 per cent there were three or more other children in the household. The large size of households was mostly accounted for by the number of children, since the majority of household structures were simple—parents (and their partner if there was one) plus children. However, nearly one in five households (19%) did include adult siblings, other relatives, or un-related members.

Going Home with Brothers and Sisters

We have seen that over two-thirds of the Protected children were committed to care along with one or more siblings. A substantial but smaller proportion were also returned home at the same time as their siblings (44%), whilst another 10 per cent had one or more siblings returned home on trial ahead of them. Thus, whilst 54 per cent of the children shared their home on trial status with at least one sibling, since 66 per cent had been committed with siblings this left at least 12 per cent of the children whose siblings were still in care when they were returned home on trial, and this is a minimum figure since a child might be returned with some siblings whilst having others still in care as well.

We found that successful home on trials were associated with placement home at the same time as siblings. Perhaps the presence of brothers and sisters offers continuity and crucial peer support and helps in the process of re-adaptation and re-absorption into the family, or possibly placement of a group of siblings represented something of a vote of confidence in the family by the social services department. These findings reflect what emerged in Berridge and Cleaver's study of foster care. They found a higher rate of success where children were placed with some or all of their siblings than where they were placed alone although having siblings in care.[5] It was interesting to discover that 62 per cent of the children from residential care were placed home on trial with (or after) siblings as opposed to 45 per cent of the children from foster placements. This would suggest that residential care had often been used to accommodate sibling groups.

*   *   *

Our evidence therefore indicated that considerable attention should be paid to both the existing composition of the households to which children returned and to the new composition that their arrival, with or without a sibling, created. In light of this not only was it surprising to find household data so poorly recorded but also that changes in household composition were rarely given as the key consideration in allowing a child home. In only 10 instances (6%) was this apparently the primary reason for the return, although in a further 10 per cent of cases it was a contributory factor. In line with the lack of household data the records also suggested that little attention was paid to a child's relationship with members of the household other than the main parent figure. From our evidence this appears to be a disquieting omission.

We were unable to monitor the subsequent changes in the composition of the home on trial households once the child had returned. Had we been able to do so the information would have been likely to have cast further light upon the fortunes of the placements. It is clearly something that needs to be undertaken in a systematic way. A good basis might be a requirement that at least at the six-monthly review a standardised statement of the prevailing household composition should be provided and significant changes (or the absence of change) considered. It will not always be a straightforward task since people come and go, disappear and reappear or are occasional members of the household. Nevertheless, we came to believe that household composition was such an important basic item of information that it should always be carefully recorded and kept up to date.

Notes and references

1. See also other studies, such as Millham *et al.*, (1986), *op. cit.* and J. Packman, *op. cit.*
2. Parker (1966), *op. cit.*
3. George, *op. cit.*
4. Berridge and Cleaver, *op. cit.*
5. *Ibid.*

CHAPTER 8

Why Home on Trial Placements were Made

It was important to discover what led to the placement of children at home on trial. As we have seen, there was one group for whom this was relatively straightforward. These were the children who either had not been removed or who had experienced a short period in care under an interim care order but who were living back with their families by the time that the full order was made. For the remainder information was gathered on the plans or intentions for their futures that were recorded on file within six months of the making of the court order or the start of the last period of voluntary care during which a parental rights resolution was made. We used this information to begin our exploration of why home on trial placements were made because they are commonly described and explained as a deliberate step in the progression towards the discharge of a care order or the rescission of a parental rights resolution; that is, a step towards the complete restoration of the child to his or her family. This implies that a conditional return forms part of a plan which has been worked out beforehand and is being overseen by a social services department. However, although our evidence indicated that this was broadly what had happened in about half the cases it was not what had happened in the rest. We discuss first what we discovered about early planning and planning in general and then consider the other major influences that led to children being allowed home.

[53]

The Influence of Planning

By the end of six months of their time in care rehabilitation had been planned for a third of the children, and if we include those for whom return home was to depend upon the progress made by one or other of the parents or by the child, the proportion for whom rehabilitation was intended rises to half. In contrast, it was noteworthy that it was considered very unlikely that a fifth of the children would ever return home and long-term placement—including in three cases adoption—was signified as the desirable goal. However, as well as these two groups there was another, comprising a third of the children, for whom there were still no plans on file after six months.[1] It is interesting to compare this with Packman's finding that no goals were clear at the outset for half the children on compulsory care orders in her study.[2]

The following table gives details of the plans that were recorded within the first six months of their care for the children in our Protected group.

Table 16. Plans recorded by six months after the child was committed to care (or within six months of the start of the period of voluntary care during which a parental rights resolution was made)
(Children not removed from home at the outset are excluded.[3] In five cases information was ambiguous)

	%
Rehabilitation planned	32
Rehabilitation possible dependent on the circumstances	18
Rehabilitation excluded	18
No clear plan made	32
	100
	N = 141

Initial plans for rehabilitation were twice as often recorded for children on whom the local authority had obtained care orders as a result of neglect or abuse[4] (43%) than for children on orders that arose from divorce or related proceedings (20%). These figures need to be treated with caution since the number of children subject to matrimonial care orders was relatively small. However, it appears that rehabilitation may be more actively considered in cases where the local authority has initiated the proceedings by which children are committed to care. Whatever the reason, it suggests that closer attention needed to be paid to planning the futures of children coming into care via the divorce courts, a route which will be altered when the 1989 Children Act is implemented.

There were signs that cases of abuse were being accorded more attention than other categories.[5] For instance, the existence of recorded plans was significantly related to the reasons for which compulsory care had been taken. Thus, rehabilitation was planned at the outset (that is within six months) for 44 per cent of the children who were in care on the grounds of abuse but for only 23 per cent of those who were in care because of neglect. Part of this difference is accounted for by the high proportion (61%) of rehabilitation plans made for the children who were siblings of an abused child. Abused children themselves were expected to be rehabilitated in 35 per cent of cases. Nonetheless, there is a suggestion in these figures that there was assumed to be a better chance of rehabilitation if a child had been abused (and especially for children who were the siblings of an abused child) than if the child had been subject to a lack of physical care or inadequate supervision. It may be that neglect has come to be regarded as more wilful and chronic than abuse; that abusing parents are seen as more motivated to work towards their child's return than neglectful parents;[6] or that the positive policies directed towards the rehabilitation of abused children are not being applied so often to neglected children. Yet, as we have seen, in practice there is a great deal of overlap between the two groups and the risk of problems recurring is not dissimilar.

This evidence suggests that the existence of some form of recorded plan or intention was connected with the requirements of child abuse procedures and, as we shall see later, this connection was confirmed. It appears that for children not subject to such procedures carefully recorded planning is less common, and it may be that professional and public preoccupation with abuse leads to other cases being given less time and attention. If this is so it is a serious matter of priorities that should be recognised and confronted as a policy issue.

The child's age when the compulsory order was made also seemed to have an important influence on planning, since six months after committal to care rehabilitation was planned for almost half (47%) of the children who were under two at the outset, but for only 28 per cent of those who were two or over. The absence of a clear plan became more common the older the child. This suggests that not only was there less careful planning in non-abuse cases but that there was a similar tendency with respect to older children.

It must be made plain that these early records of objectives might be only statements of intention rather than fully-fledged plans of action and that they hardly ever specified the period within which rehabilitation was to be achieved. It appears that social workers were anxious not to tie themselves to firm dates. This is borne out in Sinclair's report on the setting up of a computerised child care system in the Leicestershire social services department.[7] In 70 per cent of cases social workers did not state their objectives in the initial phase and they avoided the use of the categories 'restoration to the natural parents within 6 months/12 months/18 months/24 months'. They commented that they found these intervals too precise.

In our study the early plans turned out to be extremely important since they were significantly associated with the amount of time children spent in care before going home on trial. Thus 82 per cent of the children for whom firm plans for rehabilitation had been made within six months went home on trial within one year compared with 32 per cent of the children whose rehabilitation was to depend on progress made, 21 per cent of those for whom no plans had been made, and just 9 per cent of the children whose return had initially been excluded. In addition, as might be expected from the fact that plans were more often made for them, abused children got home more swiftly than neglected children. For example, 29 per cent of the abused children returned home within six months by contrast with only 16 per cent of those who had been neglected.[8]

Of course, it is not possible to say whether children arrived home sooner because their rehabilitation prospects were correctly assessed to be good or because such planning was associated with purposeful efforts to effect reunion, although Gottesfeld's work in the USA suggests the latter.[9] Similarly, the slow return of children for whom no plans had been made may have been because they were allowed to drift in care or it may have reflected the chaotic and uncertain state of their families. However, Vernon and Fruin found that many children 'remained in care or in a particular placement, not as the result of an explicit decision that this would be the best course of action, but by default',[10] and Fisher and his colleagues concluded that 'a good number of discharge processes (according to both families and social workers) occurred without the active involvement of the social workers'.[11] Millham and his team also concluded that when social workers expected children to stay in care a long time, or when they felt unable to predict what would happen, children were often destined to lengthy periods in care.[12] In view of this kind of evidence it seems likely that an active intention to achieve rehabilitation gets children home sooner than a 'wait and see' approach. Furthermore, as we have seen, the shorter the period of separation the better the outcome during home on trial but of course, as we cautioned earlier, this may reflect an accurate assessment of which children and which families can be safely re-united.

Obstacles to Return

Indeed, the case histories suggested that some children spent very long periods in care before being returned home on trial because there was great uncertainty about the ability of the family to care for the child. It has been seen that whilst children were away family structures changed rapidly, cohabitations were made and broken, and families struggled to reconstitute themselves. It was sometimes difficult to predict the course of a parent's illness, mental or physical, or of their drink or drugs problem. This could make planning for the child very difficult, especially as at times parents were themselves uncertain whether and when, if at all, they would be able to have the child home. Social workers were further hampered in their efforts if it had not been possible to secure a suitable substitute care placement for the child or if the placement made had broken down.

Nonetheless, planning in uncertainty is the reality of much social work and it was important that some planning took place that was active rather than simply reactive, and that contingency plans were made in case arrangements did not work.[13] There were some notable occasions when the social services departments took a firm stand after a period of uncertainty and thereby effected the child's return home on trial. For example, infants David and Wayne had been subject to a parental rights resolution for 18 months with no prospect of their mother having them back. The social worker then put limits on their mother's visits and told her that long-term placement was under consideration. As a result she agreed to a programme of phased rehabilitation and with the help of her sister the children returned home on trial successfully. However, exactly why some parents hesitate or are reluctant to take steps to have their children back is unclear. We should not impute a lack of interest or affection: lack of confidence and of personal support are likely to be much more common.

Some children's stays in care were protracted because the local authority was unwilling to return the child until the outcome of a hearing in the divorce court.[14] Other delays arose when a child's return home on trial was made contingent on the family's move to more suitable accommodation or the provision of a school placement. The case files contained many letters from social workers to housing and education departments pressing their clients' needs. However, there was little evidence that the fact that suitable provision would enable a child to return from care secured any priority. In particular, efforts to obtain a suitable school placement were sometimes frustrated over very long periods. During this time a child might either stay in care and suffer unnecessary separation or could be returned home and not attend school, with the accompanying educational disadvantage and pressures on the family. The report of the inquiry into the death of Tyra Henry pins responsibility firmly on local authorities to ensure that their different departments do work together in order to fulfil their corporate responsibility towards such children.[15] After all, it is the local authorities to whose care children are committed, not social services departments.

Thus, getting children home required that the family was viable and motivated or at least willing to have the child back; that obstacles to return could be surmounted, and that a suitable placement in care could be found and would hold until this was achieved. Not surprisingly, keeping all these balls in the air at once was a complicated juggling act that many social workers, for all their efforts, were unable to perform.

However, one theme which ran through many of the children's cases was the lack of clarity about what needed to happen for the child to be placed home on trial. Linked to this there was often uncertainty about the purpose of compulsory care, and what the child's stay in care was intended to achieve. Presumably social services departments needed to feel reassured that risks had diminished in relation to the grounds for compulsory care, whether these were abuse, neglect or family breakdown. However, it was rarely clear what would be taken to constitute such a reduced risk, and it was rarely spelled out in terms of the changes in behaviour or circumstances that were required.

Clearly this is an extremely difficult assessment to make. Social workers are not informed by a vast body of research as to how they might proceed and they may feel that a lack of specificity gives them valuable room for manoeuvre. Nonetheless, if greater attention were given to setting out what needed to happen for a child to go home, all interested parties—parent, child, social worker and placement care-giver—would have a better idea where they stood and, more importantly, what needed to be done.[16] A lack of clarity on these issues is likely to lead to unnecessary drift for children in care and subsequently to situations developing where they return home as the result of irresistible pressures rather than by deliberate design. This was highlighted by the situation of some children who stayed in care for long periods. As time wore on the need for a decision on the child's long-term future sometimes led to a reconsideration of home on trial to a family situation that had previously been regarded as unsuitable. This was particularly likely to happen if children were in residential care or if any kind of placement broke down so that the stability offered to the child in care was no longer assured.[17]

The Mosaic of Reasons for Return

The plans or intentions recorded by social workers within the first six months of care were important, but they were not the whole story. Families fragmented and re-grouped beyond the influence of social services departments. A child's eventual return home came about as the outcome of an interplay of forces in which social services' planning played a part but in which the actions and views of the child, the parent or relatives, and sometimes foster parents or residential homes' staff became increasingly important as time went on. In general, however, as would be expected, contact, or renewed contact between the child in care and a parent appeared to be a crucial precursor to a child's return.[18]

In those situations in which any former planning had lost its momentum, or where there were no clear intentions about the child's future, the child or the parents often stepped in and exerted pressure for restoration. Sometimes too an irresistible push for return was provided by the impossibility of maintaining a substitute care placement. This could be the result of a placement breakdown, or occasionally when foster parents or residential staff pressed for a home on trial placement;[19] or it could even be the result of a policy decision within a social services department that new initiatives were required to deal with children who seemed to be languishing in care for too long. Sometimes renewed parental visits destabilised a placement and led to pressure for home on trial.

Of course, the reasons why a home on trial placement is made are complicated and in our study the extent to which we could tease them out was limited by the fact that we were working principally with case file material. In only three-fifths of the files in our sample of Protected children were the reasons for home on trial clearly recorded. In the remainder, it was necessary to piece together the information from reviews, case conferences, case notes, court reports and other documents. Usually the standard forms on file did not call for information on the reason for a home on trial placement and at times social workers may have chosen not to record 'negative' reasons for such placements; for example, when there was no better alternative on offer in the care system or when the closure of a residential home had led to the move.

By the time that the children actually went home on trial the principal reason for half the placements appeared to be that a return was planned and followed through. However, over a third of the returns appeared to have taken place primarily as the result of pressure exerted by the parent or child, but also as a consequence of difficulties in the placement, or sometimes because of a court recommendation. For about 12 per cent of the children in the Protected group the placement was primarily the outcome of what were considered to be favourable changes in the family. Sometimes there was judged to have been a real improvement in the parent's ability to offer a home or to look after the child; for example, as a result of increased maturity or stability or an improvement in the mental health or alcohol problem of a parent. In other cases there had been a change in the composition of the household which made the family safer for the child, often because of the absence of an abusing adult. Table 17 gives the breakdown of the principal groups of reasons for the home on trial placements. The distribution is fairly similar to that obtained in a small unpublished study of home on trial undertaken by Cooper in Sheffield.[20]

Table 17. The Primary Reason for the Home on Trial Placements
(No information on two cases)

	%
Planned rehabilitation	50
Pressure from parent, child, or from within the placement or from the court	35
Changes in the family situation	12
Stage or age reached	2
Other	1
	100
	N = 170

However, home on trial placements were often made for more than one reason. The biggest secondary contributor to such placements was 'pressure'. This was a supplementary reason for home on trial for as many as 44 per cent of the Protected children.

Pressures for Return

It is by looking at the primary and secondary reasons for home on trial together that we gain the best understanding of how placements came about. This shows that the placements of two-thirds (62%) of the children were affected by 'external pressures'. Of these, the children themselves exerted the influence in over a third of the cases (for example, by asking to return or showing a high level of distress at the separation), closely followed by the parents pressing to get their children back, sometimes with the threat of an application to court to discharge the order. (In the latter cases the social services department would sometimes then agree to a placement home on trial in exchange, as it were, for retaining the control offered by the care order. In many of these situations parents did not then proceed with the application to discharge the care order, or withdrew their application). Just under a quarter of the returns that were affected by pressures were the result of the breakdown of a previous placement or its unsuitability. For the remainder of the children (8%) events during the court proceedings were influential in securing their return home.

These findings are similar to those reported by Thoburn.[21] She concluded that the most important factor in the decision to let children go home on trial was the determination of parents and children to stay together. When we analysed the large group of home on trial placements that was affected in some way by 'external' pressures we found that in something under two-thirds of them the local authority was not planning to return the child at the time that it actually happened. The points at which pressure to return a child home mounts were determined by a number of factors. In the first place it is important to note that of the placements which were affected by what we have termed 'pressure', that pressure occurred for two-thirds of them after over two years in care. It is not, surprising, of course, that return under pressure is more liable to occur when children have been in care for some time. The longer they are away the more likely it is that placements will become untenable, that parents and children will become restless about reunion and that the less contentious returns will have taken place.

However, pressures often did not come singly and when events converged there could be a build-up which was irresistible. For example, if the child was presenting difficult behaviour in care such that there was a high risk of a placement breaking down (which was compounded if a sibling group was involved) and the parent was threatening to apply for the discharge of the care order, then the arguments against home on trial could be severely undermined. Joe and his brother Lee were a case in point. As a baby Lee had 'failed to thrive' and both children were removed on care orders at the ages of four and two respectively when burns were found on them. They were strangers to discipline and their disturbed behaviour proved more than a match for a succession of care placements. During their sixth placement in a children's home, which came to the point of breakdown, their mother made an unsuccessful application to discharge the care order and their grandmother pushed for the children's return. Despite grave doubts on the part of the social services department and firm opposition from the police and other agencies about making a home on trial placement, the boys went home to their mother when Joe was seven and Lee five. The social worker noted on file in explanation of the decision that the children 'deserve a chance of rehabilitation' and, in some desperation, that 'such a course of action has to be tried'. In fact, the placement only lasted a few months before it broke down.

This case illustrates the way in which the compounding of pressures may force a local authority's hand, especially where children present such disturbed behaviour that they cannot readily be contained in care. In these circumstances some home on trial placements are clearly 'the best of a bad job' affairs and an indication of the limitations of the care system rather than a step taken because of the favourable prospects for the child at home. Even so, they may still he regarded as (and in some cases actually be) the least detrimental option by the time that so much else has been tried and failed.

The children themselves exerted pressure to return home in different ways and social services departments responded in different ways. For example, there were children who would not accept being in care and among them were those with very strong attachments[22] to their parents—attachments which could survive quite long separations. On occasion a home on trial placement was made so that a child's idealised picture of a parent could he tested against the reality. This can be an essential step to take.[23] Ashley was a case in point.[24] He was brought up by his grandmother until she died. He then joined his mother her new husband and their three children. Scapegoated and rejected by both parent figures he was removed at the age of ten because of injuries inflicted by his stepfather. Nonetheless, Ashley steadfastly maintained that he wanted to live with his mother and did not settle in any of his substitute care placements. A child psychiatrist who saw him because of his disturbed behaviour recommended that Ashley should have more contact with his mother so that he could learn for himself about the realities of their relationship in order to reach a point where he might be free to make other attachments. Regular contact with his mother was established followed by a short home on trial placement. When that failed Ashley was able to settle away from home whilst nevertheless maintaining daily contact with his family.

Other pressures upon social services departments to return a child home on trial originated in the courts, or more generally within the context of the legal system. We have seen already that in some cases a parent's threat to initiate proceedings to discharge an order may be enough to persuade social services departments to agree to return children home on trial. In other cases a similar bargaining process takes place under the auspices of the court. There were six children for whom proceedings in court appeared to be influential in getting them placed home on trial. In one case a magistrate had agreed to make a care order on the understanding that the children would be returned home on trial at once, and a memorandum to this effect was on the file. There were another five children whom the local authority wished to place in long-term care, but instead placed home on trial because it was considered that the evidence for long-term care away from the parents would not withstand scrutiny during the further legal proceedings that it was likely to engender.

Obviously, some kinds of pressure may be beneficial and an indication of the eagerness of the child and parents to resume living together. However, we found that those placements that had been brought about *primarily* by outside pressures such as we have described (just over a third of them) were significantly less successful than those which were principally the result of a planned return or favourable changes in the family situation.

As we have seen, the main reasons for a child returning home were combined with an assortment of secondary reasons, so that planning, pressures and changes in the families' situation were often interwoven in complicated ways. Only a little over a fifth (22%) of the cases broadly conformed to what might be regarded as the simple model of rational planning; that is, cases where the social services department made a confident decision for home on trial (sometimes in consultation with the parents) and was able to maintain the initiative for return at about the time that it was intended untroubled by outside impingements. The pure 'planned rehabilitations' of the textbooks were the exception rather than the rule.

Changes in the Family Situation and Return

Thus, most placements home on trial were made as a result of a planned move on the part of a social department or as a consequence of outside pressures, or a combination of the two. It was less common to find that changes in the family's situation were the reason for the return home. When we add to the 12 per cent of children for whom it was a principal reason the 18 per cent for whom it was the secondary reason, we find that this was the case in only just under a third of the placements. In over half of them the changes in question were improvements in family functioning such that the parent(s) were in a better position to care for the child. In a quarter improvements in housing assisted the placement and in nearly a fifth it was the exclusion of an adult who was considered to endanger the child.

What is striking about these figures is that changes in a family's situation played a comparatively small part in determining the decision for return, even taking primary and secondary reasons together. Indeed, in reading the case files we were surprised to find so little evidence for any change in the perceived quality of family relationships. By and large good relationships remained good and poor ones poor, albeit with some notable exceptions.

This may well constitute a major dilemma for social workers and others in deciding whether or not to make a home on trial placement. They need to be able to believe in the possibility of change for families and yet live with the reality that it is very difficult to achieve. As Dingwall and his colleagues put it: 'staff are required, if possible, to think the best of parents'.[25] What was worrying was the number of occasions when social workers wrote unrealistically about aiming to achieve change, when the child and family's history—if looked at as a whole—should have made it clear that this was unlikely to happen. In relation to rehabilitation, Wolkind refers to 'therapeutic over-optimism concerning the amount of change that intervention can bring about in a family'.[26]

This emphasis on achieving change is obviously an important theme in social work, since it is an underlying rationale for much of what is done. However, more research is needed on what can and cannot change, by the application of which resources and under what circumstances.[27] Yet with such a dominating rationale it is not surprising that changes in one area coupled with greater co-operation from parents may be mistaken for more far-reaching changes.[28] For example, a social worker who had assisted in getting a family rehoused wrote that they had 'moved a great deal' in their attitude to the children. However when the children—one of whom had been seriously abused—were returned home on trial the stepfather's violent behaviour re-emerged as a source of continuing concern: housing was not the key issue.

It was also noticeable that when social workers carried responsibility for children whose family circumstances were considered to be barely satisfactory, the case reviews sometimes failed to acknowledge the dilemmas inherent in their position. For example, after five years of contact with parents who drank heavily, were aggressive and threatening, the social worker wrote in a review of the home on trial placement that his aim was 'to continue as far as practicable to work with this family and to influence a change in attitudes and handling of the children'. It might have been more realistic either to face up to how unsatisfactory the placement was and take action, or to acknowledge that change would be unlikely to take place and justify continuation of the placement for other reasons and support it with other kinds of help and resources.

These examples raise the issue of the *realistic* assessment of (a) the likelihood of critical behaviour being changed, (b) whether any such change can be sustained over time and (c) if that likelihood is low, whether other kinds of resources can be deployed which improve the situation of the child sufficiently for damage to be contained. In making such an assessment it is not enough to concentrate upon what happens between the principal carer and the child. The risk may be a function of the relationship between the adults in the household and of their relative power. The problem for a caring mother may be the behaviour of her partner, especially his behaviour towards the child. In that sense, the discussion of parent-child relationships as if they were one-dimensional is almost certainly a dangerous simplification. Matters are often more complicated and assessments difficult to make. That being so it is important to re-emphasise the fact that alterations in household composition are one of the changes that are most likely to lead to a different quality of relationships, one way or another. Social workers face monumental problems in endeavouring to modify the quality of long-established relationships or their consequences, especially without specialised therapeutic resources. Nor can they engineer the rearrangement of households (except in some instances by recourse to the courts). What they can do, however, is to monitor very carefully the changes in household composition (both adults and children) and assess the impact of these changes upon the care that a child is likely to receive or be receiving.

* * *

Authorisation for Return and Consultation with other Agencies

In the paragraphs above we have referred rather loosely to 'social workers' with reference to their decisions and judgements. Of course, most decisions are complicated affairs and it is rare for any one person's influence to reign supreme. That was certainly true for the decisions to allow children home on trial. Nevertheless, there is a point at which the decision (even though it be the ratification of what has already happened) is formally made or formally approved. As we have seen the new Charge and Control regulations now oblige directors of social service to make these formal decisions or to nominate (in writing) a senior colleague at act on their behalf. No such requirements existed during the period of our study and we were therefore interested to establish at what level the formal decision to allow a child home on trial was made. For this we relied upon the record on file. One authority had a special form for requesting authority for home on trial placements with spaces for the signatures of the team leader, principal social worker and area officer. In the other authorities it was necessary to rely on recorded membership of case conferences prior to the placement and signatures on six-monthly review forms or the occasional case note or memorandum indicating discussion of the placement with a social work manager. We found that 44 per cent of the placements were authorised at or above principal social worker/area director level,[29] whilst well over a third (37%) were agreed by team leaders. For nearly one in five (19%) the decision was apparently taken at field level. Table 18 gives the breakdown.

Table 18. The Level of Authorisation for the Home on Trial Placements
(For 8 cases the information was unavailable or ambiguous)

	%	
Field social worker	19	
Team leader	37	
Area Director/Principal social worker	40	
More senior manager	4	
	100	N = 164

The level of authorisation was one of the few variables on which the four local authorities showed considerable difference. None of them had a written policy about home trial authorisation in 1984. However, one was definite that it lay at area director level (or with a named delegate of the area director). Two others 'expected' authorisation to be at principal social worker/area director level. Only one authority had considered that authorisation should be given by team leaders.[30] In practice, in two of the local authorities decisions had been authorised at area director level or higher in two-thirds of the cases. One was the local authority where this was both a requirement and where a well-organised system for six-monthly reviews was in place. The other was the one with a special form used to authorise placements. In contrast, in the authority with expectations but no form only 28 per cent of the placements were apparently authorised at area director level and in the one where team leader level sufficed, only 16 per cent were taken above that level. When we looked specifically at the return of abused children across all four local authorities we found that the proportion of placements authorised at area director level or above rose to 57 per cent of all such placements. This left over a third (36%) of abused children who were returned with a team leader's agreement and 7 per cent where the decision appeared to rest with the field social worker.

It can be seen that four out of five of all the decisions for home on trial for Protected children were shared upwards within the social services department hierarchy. How far then did the social services departments share their responsibilities for making the placements with other agencies? A case conference or residential review was held at which the home on trial placement was discussed in over half of the Protected cases. For 45 per cent of them however there was no such meeting prior to the placement. The likelihood of such a meeting taking place was closely linked to where the child was placed. In nearly 70 per cent of the residential placements a review or case conference was held prior to home on trial, but a meeting of interested parties only happened in just over a quarter (28%) of the cases of children in foster homes. This is similar to the finding of the Social Work Service in their study of the boarding-out of children,[31] where it was discovered that the reviews of children in residential establishments were accorded more importance, and were held more regularly, than those for children in foster homes.

We sought information on who attended case conferences and residential reviews for that half of the children for whom such a meeting was held prior to their return. However, in 16 cases although there was a meeting there was no information about who attended. At other times such information was partial and names were given but not job designations, so that an outsider or newcomer within the social services department would not be reliably informed about attendance. On the whole, information about attendance was fuller for case conferences than for residential reviews.

Where a multidisciplinary meeting was held attendance could be established, at least in part, in 80 cases (46%). Residential staff attended nearly three-quarters of the meetings (71%). Foster parents only attended in six cases. A teacher was present for 40 per cent of the meetings but that was usually a teacher from the residential establishment or the local school. It was very rare for a teacher to attend from the school which the child would attend once home on trial. Health visitors or their managers attended in 44 per cent of cases (and this included almost all of the meetings on children under five) but general practitioner attendance was a rarity. Police were present at 35 per cent of the meetings. The attendance by other professionals like hospital doctors, educational psychologists or legal officers of the local authority was uncommon. Finally, the parent or parent figures to whom the children were likely to go home on trial were present at only 6 per cent of the meetings and the children themselves attended in only 10 cases (6%).

Thus, it appears that decisions about home on trial were shared upwards within social services departments far more often than they were shared outwards to involve other agencies. Least of all were the parents or children themselves formally involved in these decisions.[32] This may be relevant in considering the extent to which parents and children with limited access to the formal decision processes make their views felt by exerting pressure for the return in other ways. At the time of our study this low level of parental participation was apparently persisting in spite of a growing body of opinion that parents should be formally involved in all decisions regarding their child. Such views had been expressed in reports published by the British Association of Social Workers, the Family Rights Group, the Children's Legal Centre, and the National Council for One Parent Families.[33]

However, decisions were not always straightforward and agreement at case conferences was not always reached. In as many as a third of the cases (32%) concern was recorded about the decision to make a home on trial placement. In 15 per cent of the cases this involved the reservations of social services staff alone, and in 9 per cent of the cases their reservations were echoed by those of other professionals. In 8 per cent of the cases the concern was that of other professionals alone. Interestingly, the placements which were significantly least successful were those about which reservations were expressed by members of the social services department itself.

Social services departments are now obliged by regulations to inform education and certain health authorities about the placement of a child home on trial. When our study was undertaken no such requirement existed. It is interesting therefore (and a valuable point for future comparison) to see that at the time of our study other agencies were not alerted to the fact that a child was going home on trial on a routine basis; or at least no evidence of a communication appeared on file. The exceptions were individual area offices within two of the local authorities which used former children's department procedures and regularly circulated both the education department and the general practitioner about all home on trial placements. We found that in just over half of the Protected cases information about the child's return had probably not been shared with the education department or the child's general practitioner, even though two-thirds of the children were subject to orders for abuse or neglect.

Before leaving the issue of the extent and nature of participation in the decisions about placements home on trial we must emphasise that the study only looked at those which led to a child's return. It may be that decisions not to allow a home on trial placement followed a different pattern. Some may have been more controversial and therefore more often referred upwards; some may have been the result of successful opposition by representatives of other agencies at a case conference, whilst others may have been the outcome of a general agreement amongst several organisations that it was unwise to permit a child to go home, even on a trial basis.

Notes and references

1. Similarly, Sinclair (1984, *op. cit.*) found that there were no stated plans or objectives with respect to three-quarters of the 396 case files that she examined in her study of reviews. However, these included children in voluntary care.
2. Packman, *op. cit.*

3. In this case we have excluded all the children not removed from home at the outset and not merely those who were not subsequently removed (see note 1, chapter 5).

4. It is important to remember (see Chapter 5) that the majority of cases of abuse were *physical abuse*. There were very few cases of sexual abuse.

5. Children subject to parental rights resolutions were especially likely to have no clear plan made for their future within six months (52%). This was probably in part because we calculated their periods in care from the start of the last episode of voluntary care during which the parental rights resolution was made. As a result, within six months many of the children would still have been in voluntary care. Even when we exclude children subject to parental rights resolutions there were still 27 per cent of children in the Protected group for whom no clear plan was recorded within six months. This is a worrying state of affairs but one which may have improved since the time of our study, given the greater prominence of child abuse cases and more central government guidance.

6. This point is made by P. Crittenden in 'Family Dyadic Patterns of Functioning in Maltreating Families' in K. Browne, C. Davies and P. Stratton (eds), *Early Prediction and Prevention of Child Abuse*, Wiley and Sons, 1988.

7. R. Sinclair, 'Recording Social Work Objectives', in *Research, Policy and Planning*, vol. 5, no. 2, 1988.

8. Similarly, in the Dartington Social Research Unit's study of place of safety orders, a higher proportion of neglected children than abused children were still in care after two years. Dartington Social Research Unit, *Place of Safety Orders: A Study of Children Provided for Under Section 28 of the Children and Young Persons Act, 1969*. This is also evident in the cases of neglect in *Predicting Children's Length of Stay in Care and the Relevance of Family Links*, Dartington Social Research Unit, 1984.

9. H. Gottesfeld, *In Loco Parentis: A Study of Perceived Role Values in Foster Home Care*, Jewish Welfare Association, New York, 1970. This study showed that children drifted in care without firm plans because of a failure to work with parents from the outset of the care period.

10. Vernon and Fruin, *op. cit.*

11. M. Fisher, P. Marsh, D. Phillips and E. Sainsbury, *In and Out of Care: the Experiences of Children, Parents and Social Workers*, Batsford, 1986.

12. Millham *et al.* (1986), *op. cit.*

13. See, R. A. Parker, 'Planning into Practice', in *Adoption and Fostering*, vol. 9. no. 4, 1985.

14. This can be compared with the delays which sometimes occur in completing care proceedings when there is a criminal case against the

parents. See, E. Farmer and R. A. Parker, *A Study of Interim Care Orders*, Department of Social Administration, University of Bristol, 1985, and M. Murch and L. Mills, *The Length of Care Proceedings*, research connected with the study of the Representation of the Child in Civil Proceedings, undertaken for the DHSS, Socio-Legal Centre for Family. Studies, University of Bristol, 1987.

15. *Whose Child? The Report of the Panel Appointed to Inquire into the Death of Tyra Henry*, London Borough of Lambeth, 1987.

16. The importance to parents for such issues to be made clear is shown in C. Brown, *Child Abuse Parents Speaking: A Consumer Study*, School for Advanced Urban Studies, Working Paper 63, University of Bristol, 1984. In this study the issue addressed was that parents of abused children needed to know exactly what was required of them for their children to be removed from the child abuse register. When parents did not know what was expected of them they felt very uncomfortable and confused during social work visits.

17. See also Vernon and Fruin, *op. cit.* The authors comment on returns home in these circumstances. Such returns were considered by social workers to represent only 'a less detrimental alternative for the child to that of remaining in care'.

18. See also Aldgate, *op. cit.* and Fanshel (1975), *op. cit.*

19. Vernon and Fruin, *op. cit.* In this study they describe the part which placement care-givers played in returning children home both when foster placements broke down and when residential staff pressed for a non-residential placement or demanded a child's removal. See also, Thoburn (1980), *op. cit.* This study found that social workers were influenced by the views of placement care-givers about whether children should go home. Aldgate, *op. cit.*, found that parents' contact with their children was greatly influenced by the attitude of the care-takers towards the parents.

20. R.A. Cooper, *A Study of Children 'Trial-Own-Parent' Subjects of Care Orders under the 1969 Children and Young Persons Act in Sheffield*, 1982 (unpublished). Of the reasons recorded for home on trials in Sheffield in 1981, 40 per cent were planned rehabilitations, 20 per cent were made because of a placement breakdown, and 20 per cent because of pressure from parent(s) or because of changes in the situation of the parent or child.

21. Thoburn (1980), *op. cit.* Thoburn added that: 'where social work plans changed, it was usually in response to pressure from the parents and/or children, or to the unhappiness of the children when away from home'.

22. Consideration of where a child's attachments lie is clearly crucial in making decisions about the future. There was a small group of children who had formed their primary attachment not to a parent but to a substitute care-giver in consequence of living in their family from a young age. For these children placement with a birth parent some years later involved relinquishing such attachments, sometimes with severe consequences. Children in this situation could experience especially acute problems of adjustment with accompanying behaviour disturbance and present a formidable challenge to the coping skills of what was often a reconstituted family. Yet if the home on trial placement broke down under the strain, as it was liable to do, the child was left with a double loss. The original foster families were rarely able to take the child back.

23. E. Fein, A.N. Maluccio, J. Hamilton and D.E. Ward, 'After Foster Care: Permanency Planning for Children', in *Child Welfare, 62, (6), 1983*. This study found that of children 'stuck' in the care system, those for whom rehabilitation was tried settled more successfully even if they were eventually placed with permanent substitute families.

24. Names and minor details, in this and subsequent case examples, have been altered to preserve confidentiality.

25. R. Dingwall, J. Eekelaar and R. Murray, *The Protection of Children*, Blackwell, 1983.

26. S. Wolkind, *The Mental Health of Children in Care—Research Needs*, Economic and Social Research Council, 1988.

27. An example of such a study is that by A. Rushton, J. Treseder and D. Quinton, *New Parents for Older Children*, British Agencies for Adoption and Fostering, 1988. This study of 18 older children separates out behaviours which did and did not change in the first year of the children's substitute family placements.

28. Social Services Inspectorate, *Inspection of the Supervision of Social Workers in the Assessment and Monitoring of Cases of Child Abuse when Children Subject to a Court Order have been Returned Home*, DHSS, 1986. This issue was the subject of comment in this report on 117 abused children returned home on trial. It was noted with some concern that decisions for returns were 'sometimes based on the availability of support services rather than on changes in the family and their ability to care for the child'.

29. It should be noted that the hierarchies in our four local authorities varied considerably and equivalence was not always easy to establish.

30. Interestingly, in the days of the children's departments, authorisation in this local authority had been at area director level.

31. Social Work Service, *A Study of the Boarding-Out of Children*, DHSS, 1981.

32. The lack of involvement of parents in the crucial decisions that affected their children was a feature of the Cleveland situation. The Cleveland report recommended that parents should be invited to attend case conferences. *Report of the Inquiry into Child Abuse in Cleveland 1987*, Cm 412, HMSO, 1988.

33. British Association of Social Workers, *Clients are Fellow Citizens*, 1980; Family Rights Group, *The Three R's of Social Work*, a submission to the National Institute for Social Work Inquiry, 1981; Children's Legal Centre, *Evidence to the NISW Committee*, 1981; National Council for One-Parent Families, *Inquiry into Social Work—Evidence to the NISW Committee*, 1981.

CHAPTER 9

Supporting the Placements: Ambiguity and Uncertainty

Social Work and Other Resources

The purpose of a 'trial' placement would seem to be to determine whether or not children should be restored to their families on a permanent basis. That, however, poses a major question about the amount and kind of help that families should be offered during the trial. Can their competence and safety be adequately judged if, for example, they receive a great deal of help and supervision which is liable to be reduced or withdrawn once the trial is considered to have been satisfactorily completed? In short, to what extent is support a distorting variable in the assessment if it is not to be continued on a permanent basis or if it fails to effect a substantial change in a family's capabilities?

The Social Services Inspectorate report on abused children considered that when families received intensive services it might be difficult to assess the quality of their parenting and whether significant changes had taken place.[1] Morrison and Dale, in separate publications reporting on the work of the specialist NSPCC child protection team in Rochdale[2] suggested that rehabilitation plans which depended on high levels of surveillance and community support (including full-time day nursery placements) were liable to mask the fact that parents were actually considered to be untrustworthy and unpredictable. Our study lent some support to this view. A significantly higher proportion (32%) of placements that depended on intensive help had poor or detrimental outcomes than those which did not (17%).

[73]

Public policies have often reflected a deep-seated aversion to helping parents look after their own children. Unrelated carers have usually been regarded as more eligible for assistance. Historically, the assistance that parents have received has been hedged around by a variety of explicit and implicit conditions that reflect an enduring ambiguity.[3] A strong moral component is to be found in child care practices: parents 'ought' to care for their children largely unaided and if they fail to do so they are liable to be seen as irresponsible, perverse, inadequate or unfit. Therein, we came to believe, lay an important dilemma in the management of home on trial placements and in the way in which those who were on trial viewed their contacts with social services departments. If they asked for help would it count against them?

In light of these issues we considered it important to discover what kinds of support and supervision were provided once a child was home on trial, and to what effect. It was, of course, difficult to find out everything that had happened, particularly as we relied upon the records of social services departments. Nevertheless, we believe that we obtained a reasonably accurate picture of what was provided.

We found that support services of one kind or another were arranged in 42 per cent of the Protected children's placements. This was often a day nursery placement or assistance from a family aide or home help. Indeed, the central role played by day nurseries in home on trials for the under fives is shown by the fact that three-quarters of the children in this age group attended day nursery whilst they were home on trial. Seventeen per cent of the children over eight participated in an intermediate treatment or activity group at some stage. In addition, 18 per cent of children of school age attended special school whilst they were home on trial.[4] Thus the resources most often used were those directly under the control of social services departments.

There were 18 families (10%) where it was clear that the viability of the home on trial placement depended upon the support offered by relatives, usually the grandparents. In addition, in 38 instances (22%) we considered that placements were able to be maintained *only* as the result of intensive help from outside agencies. This was almost a quarter of the Protected cases. In 18 instances this was social work help, in six it was support from a school and in 13 cases it was by a combination of support from social work and another agency (usually a day nursery or a school). One family received support from a voluntary agency.

Other agencies were recorded as being involved in monitoring children's attendance at school or nursery, or in watching for signs of abuse or neglect in the case of 40 per cent of the group of Protected children, and there was some evidence that 11 per cent of them had occasionally been monitored for weight and growth by either the health visitor or a hospital. However, there was no record of the regular monitoring of children's growth or the use of percentile charts to check on height, weight and head circumference over any period of time. These findings are consistent with those in the Social Services Inspectorate's report on the monitoring of child abuse cases, which found that health monitoring was generally lacking and that social workers were unaware of the significance of the information which could be obtained from health checks.[5] More use of percentile charts might now be made since their importance in detecting cases of abuse was emphasised in the report of the inquiry into the death of Jasmine Beckford.[6] However, it should be noted that health visitor activity is not routinely recorded on social work case file. The extent of health monitoring might have been found to have been greater had we had the resources to study health visitors' files as well.

Unfortunately, we were also handicapped in assessing the amount of social work help and supervision (interpreted as the number of face-to-face contacts made) that the families received because in many instances the records were incomplete; that is, there were gaps when either contacts had lapsed or they had failed to be noted. If little or no contact was recorded during the period home on trial but regular visits had been made before and after the placement, we took this to be an accurate record of events. Otherwise we excluded the apparently incomplete files from our analysis. On this basis just over half (52%) of the cases had to be omitted.

We used the remainder to calculate the level of social work activity. The total number of contacts with each case was divided by the number of months the placement continued in order to obtain an average frequency. Unfortunately this does not tell us about the fluctuations in patterns of contact and, because of the omitted cases, it may be slanted towards those where the worker was most active. Nonetheless, among those where records were complete, 30 per cent of the cases were visited on average less often than monthly. In this situation it is questionable what function could be served by the maintenance of compulsory powers. On the other hand, 70 per cent of the families were visited monthly or more frequently and this included a quarter who were visited on average fortnightly or more often. Since placements, as we will see, were often very long, this suggests a high level of contact. It does not, of course, include the amount of time spent writing letters, making phone calls and carrying out other administrative tasks connected with the home on trial placement. It will be recalled that almost one in five of the placements appeared highly unlikely to survive without very high levels of support from social workers. Indeed, one local authority had appointed a social worker to work with just one family.

The average visiting frequencies are shown in table 19 below.

Table 19. The Recorded Frequency of Social Work Contact with Parents/Children During Home on Trial Placement
(Incomplete record of visits for 90 cases)

	%	
No contact recorded	3	
Less than monthly	27	
Monthly—less than fortnightly	45	
Fortnightly—less than weekly	18	
Weekly or more often	7	
	100	N = 82

Whilst this tells us something about the considerable amounts of time social workers commit to these placements, it does not provide information about the quality of the work. However, the Social Services Inspectorate's report on the monitoring of abused children during home on trial commented on the frequency of social work visits after the children's return home but considered that the purpose of these visits was often unclear and that the needs of the child and those of the family were not well differentiated.[7]

We noted whether six-monthly reviews clearly documented the progress of the child during placement such that a fairly full and clear picture of the child's development emerged. This would provide some information about whether the needs of the children were being properly considered and placed in the context of their overall development. In our view a reasonably good picture of the child's progress was available in just under half the Protected cases (46%), but it was lacking in over a third (36%), whilst in nearly a fifth (18%) the quality of the documentation was variable. Clear recording of the child's progress at review, at least some of the time, was associated with successful home on trial placements. We also checked all the abuse and neglect cases (124) to see whether the file showed clearly when the child was seen. This had been the subject of comment in the Social Services Inspectorate's report[8] and in the Jasmine Beckford inquiry.[9] We found that in only 43 per cent of these cases was it consistently clear from the files whether the child had been seen during visits. We checked child abuse cases for clear documentation of the level of risk involved both in the decision to place the child home on trial and during the progress of the placement and found that risk levels were clearly recorded in just over half of them. Again we found that among the abused children, more successful home on trial placements were significantly associated with the existence of such statements.

In reading the case files, we came increasingly to the view that effective social work during home on trial was carried out when the workers were clear about the responsibility they carried in respect of the care order and about their expectations of the placement. This allowed their contact with the child and family to be purposeful. Social workers needed to be regular and persistent in making contact with families and to be able to address the changing needs of the child and family whilst maintaining a clear child-centred focus and, if necessary, to use their authority to ensure that the child's needs were met. Clarity of purpose allowed workers to have an overall view of the situation and ride out difficulties when they occurred. It was this clarity of purpose plus the ability to use their authority, combined with steady, reliable visiting, that seemed to mark out the most effective social work. The use of more specialised methods, such as family therapy or referral to child guidance, was rare.

As far as we could tell from the records, there were many examples of good practice among the placements. Occasionally a social worker seemed to lack clarity of purpose and there were odd examples of workers who were neither purposeful nor able to use their authority, and whose time was spent in running errands for their clients. In one local authority a reorganisation had taken place within the social services department in March, 1984 when our sample of placements was drawn. The management of cases in this local authority suffered from this disruption and some of the children home on trial and their families were unallocated for periods of time. In all, 25 Protected cases were unallocated at some time during home on trial, 22 from this local authority. It was very noticeable that when this happened inappropriate placements continued or children's needs were not assessed. Successful outcomes were significantly associated with a social worker being allocated to the case during the whole of the home on trial placement.

We did consider whether there were cases in which it appeared not only that the social work offered had been competent and able but that it had, in our view, also contributed positively to the course of events; that is, without it things might have been rather different. It will be readily recognised that even a very good and purposeful social work input will often not be able to influence what happens. In our opinion there were 31 Protected cases, or nearly one in five, in which the social work offered had played a major and decisive part in the way that things worked out during home on trial. This seemed to us to be an encouraging finding. These 31 cases had a high proportion of positive outcomes—84 per cent as compared with 41 per cent for other Protected cases. Furthermore, a significant proportion were cases where the order had been made on the grounds of child abuse.

It was plain, therefore, that some of the home on trial placements had had considerable social work time devoted to them, especially the abuse cases. There was also evidence that high quality work had been done. Had the case records been fuller, or more complete, we might have found that even more cases were attracting these heavy professional investments. We suspect, however, that poor or erratic recording was often associated with rather poor or disrupted social work.

Two points must be made in concluding our comments about the social work that was provided. First, it seems likely that if social work is to make a positive difference (at least for the Protected group of children) then there will have to be a heavy and purposeful investment; it is therefore unlikely to be a cheap option. Secondly, if this is so, then it raises again the questions of how far, under those circumstances, the capacities of the carers can be accurately assessed; for how long after care orders are discharged social work support will be needed and, in light of that, to what extent social work (however good it be judged to be) is able to contrive lasting changes in family relationships or circumstances.

Financial Assistance

If considerable use is made of a limited range of support services to aid home on trial placements, the same cannot be said of financial assistance. When payments were given they appeared to be made from 'section I' money. Section I of the Child Care Act, 1980 (which replaced section I of the 1963 Children and Young Persons Act) allows local authorities to provide cash if it will 'promote the welfare of children by diminishing the need to receive children into or keep them in care'. However, the eligibility of parents with children home on trial for such payments did not appear to be clear. Since they are already in care, prevention of reception into care is not possible; but presumably they can meet the criterion of diminishing the need to keep them in care or prevent them coming before the courts. The other alternative was for local authorities to use money from the larger budgets allocated specifically to children who are in care. However, there was very little evidence in our study that money from this source was used to assist children who were placed home on trial.

We collected detailed information on the payments made during home on trial in one of the local authorities. It did not appear to differ markedly from the others in its use of financial assistance. We found that cash payments were made from department funds (usually section I money) to over half the families of Protected children home on trial in that local authority. Taking both the Protected and Disaffected groups of children together for that local authority, payments were made to 47 per cent of the families where there was a home on trial placement. Fourteen families received £30 or less, and the average was just over £50 per family. In some cases this was supplemented by grants from charities. Given that most home on trial placements were of considerable duration, this did not appear unduly generous although, unlike accommodation and schooling, the local authority was able to act on their own behalf in the matter.

Indeed, the provision of financial help appeared to be a thorny issue. The local authority in question, like the others, seemed to be fairly ready to offer assistance in cash or kind to enable a home on trial placement to be made. This often involved the provision of a bed or bedding for the returning child. However, prior to placement, financial support was frequently needed in order to clear rent or fuel arrears; but this was less often forthcoming.

Once the child was placed home on trial there appeared to be a lack of agreement about the appropriateness of providing financial assistance; social work managers were sometimes reluctant to agree to payments requested by field workers. The local authority in which we collected this information used a home on trial agreement form which stated that the parent or carer agreed to be responsible for the child's maintenance. In some teams this was enforced more rigorously than in others. Thus, one social worker wrote on file:

> Informed (mother) that this payment [for shoes] would be the last and that one of the ideas behind the issue of 'home on trial' was that the family could prove they could manage with their present resources, and work around such problems without outside help.

Thus, in this case the home on trial was seen not just as a trial of parenting but also of the parents' ability to budget on a limited income. Most families in the study depended heavily upon social security benefits.

However, in some instances great efforts were made to obtain financial support. Charities were sometimes quite forthcoming and eight families received an average of £84 each from charity. One of these was a single father who, under some pressure from the social services department, gave up his longstanding job to look after his children. His social worker obtained annuities totalling £280 in an attempt to help him with his enforced drop in income. Again, it was noticeable that financial help, especially that from social services departments, was particularly likely to be provided if it directly upheld the aims of the placement or if refusing to give it might threaten its continuation. Thus, provision for clothing or even a bicycle might be made to enable a child to get to school, or when older to enable a young person to attend a youth training scheme or job interview.

There was no doubt that some families had serious financial difficulties. One of the families we interviewed felt too grateful for the return of the child and too anxious to show the social worker that they were coping, to ask for advice or help about their financial problems. Yet in this case the financial worries were the direct result of the stepfather giving up work in order to help look after the children and provide support for the mother.

In the case of relatives who have a child home on trial the situation can be quite different, since the local authority has the option of approving them as foster parents and paying a boarding-out allowance. However, practice varied considerably in this. Of the nine original home on trial placements with relatives, five were in one local authority. It was in this local authority that there was particular reluctance to convert such arrangements to foster placements with relatives. Even so, there were opposing voices within this local authority. One team manager expressed shock at hearing of these home on trial placements with relatives continuing long-term without boarding-out payments. In her view, this was a case of the local authority having children 'in care without payment'. The arguments adduced for not converting such home on trial placements to boarding-out placements were that in many cases relatives' standards would be too low to be approved by the fostering panel; that children disliked the regular medicals required by the boarding-out regulations,[10] and that it created disincentives for the discharge of the care order since payments would then be foregone. It emerged that in practice there was some flexibility over such issues and that boarding-out placements with relatives tended to be made when the local authority was anxious to make such a placement and considered that payment was the only way to obtain or keep it.

However, this meant that in some cases relatives who made it clear that they wanted to look after the children, and did not urge their poverty as a bar, were left without boarding-out payments. There was a small number of these long-term home on trial placements where grandparents were managing to offer children a satisfactory home but battling constantly to cope on low incomes. Withholding boarding-out payments from these families seemed to produce quite unnecessary hardship. In one memorable case the social worker spent a large amount of his time trying to squeeze some financial help from the social security system or from his own department for a grandmother who had two children home on trial. Most of his contact with the family centred round the grandmother's financial worries rather than around the children. The grandmother consulted a law centre whose solicitor requested that the social services department pay boarding-out allowance. The request was refused. The cost to the local authority of the worker's time spent trying to drum up small payments for the grandmother was not taken into account, much less the cost to the local authority if the placement had broken down. It was just such a situation in the case of Tyra Henry's grandmother which led to the recommendation in the inquiry report that she should have been made Tyra's foster mother, which would have given 'some desperately needed financial help, to which she was most certainly morally entitled'.[11]

The Child Care Act, 1980 states in section 21 that the local authority has a duty 'to provide accommodation and maintenance' for children under care orders whether through placement with foster parents, in a community home or by placement with a parent, guardian, relative or friend. In the inquiry report on Tyra Henry the panel argued that the wording of the Act thus places an obligation on a local authority to provide accommodation and maintenance for children home on trial and that there is therefore no problem about the more limited wording of section I of the Child Care Act which governs the making of assistance in cash or kind. It was argued in the report that 'the assumption of legal responsibility for a child brings with it the power and the duty to use all appropriate resources of the local authority to take good care of the child'.[12] It held that the local authority should have ensured that Tyra's grandmother was properly rehoused and had sufficient income to care for her.

The question of the extent to which parents or relatives looking after children who are home on trial should be helped financially continues to remain unsettled. For example, in the Handbook of Guidance that accompanied the new regulations it was pointed out that Charge and Control 'may be said to suggest an element of financial responsibility on the carer'. Furthermore, it was explained that 'although not defined the extent of delegation by the local authority to the carer should involve a degree of responsibility for a child *over and above* that which occurs when a child is placed with foster parents' (emphasis added).[13] This presumably included financial responsibility. However, under the Children Act, 1989 financial help should be available for placements with relatives and friends since these arrangements will no longer be covered by the revised regulations. Instead, they will be governed by foster placement regulations.

Of course, one of the main tensions in home on trial policies and practices derives from the different needs of the carers and the children. If parents or relatives are to care adequately for a child they will often need to be supported and helped. The children may well have different needs. Help and support that is focused on the child appears to arouse fewer misgivings than that which is offered to the parents. For example, the *Handbook of Guidance* was quite clear that the local authority has a duty to provide support for the child even after he or she leaves care.[14] Nevertheless, the prescription that a supervisor should 'differentiate between the need of the child and the carer' and then 'focus primarily on the child'[15] is easier to formulate than to put into practice.

*   *   *

For the first time the Charge and Control regulations and the revised regulations which accompany the 1989 Children Act confront the issue of the balance of responsibility that is expected in a home on trial placement. Despite that, many uncertainties remain and it seems likely that the placement agreements which are now required to be drawn up between the local authority and the carer will be framed differently for different carers. The ambiguities that have surrounded home on trial placements will continue even though they are now more clearly recognised.

Notes and references

1. Social Services Inspectorate (1986), *op. cit.*
2. T. Morrison, 'Creating Changes in Abusing Families', in *Adoption and Fostering*, vol. 11, no. 2, 1987; P. Dale, *Dangerous Families: Assessment and Treatment of Child Abuse*, Tavistock, 1986.
3. See Parker (1991), *op. cit.*
4. Special schooling was taken to include all forms of special education provided by an education department.
5. Social Services Inspectorate (1986), *op. cit.*
6. *A Child in Trust*, *op. cit.* However, the importance of baseline data on a child's growth and development was made clear earlier in the DHSS publication, *Child Abuse: A Study of Inquiry Reports 1973–1983*, HMSO, 1982.
7. Social Services Inspectorate (1986), *op. cit.*
8. *Ibid.*
9. *A Child in Trust*, *op. cit.*
10. The Charge and Control regulations require that regular medicals shall be carried out.
11. *Whose Child? op. cit.*
12. *Ibid.*
13. *Handbook of Guidance*, *op. cit.*, para. 15.
14. *Ibid.*, para. 64.
15. *Ibid.*

CHAPTER 10

Monitoring Home on Trial Placements

Reviews

Given the risks that are associated with placing children home on trial it is vital that progress is regularly reviewed, reassessments made and, if necessary, steps taken to deal with unsatisfactory situations. The main procedure by which this is achieved is the six-monthly review that has to be undertaken in respect of all children in care. The extent to which this statutory requirement is met has been found to vary within as well as between social services departments.[1] Our findings largely confirmed this state of affairs. Six-monthly reviews were recorded as having been held at the required frequency (or more often) throughout their placement home on trial for only 30 per cent of the Protected children. In nearly half the cases (48%) reviews were sometimes carried out at six-monthly intervals and sometimes not, and in somewhat more than a fifth (22%) they never met the statutory requirement. Quite long periods could elapse without a review taking place. Approaching half (46%) of all the children had at least one gap of over a year between reviews.

However, the frequency of the reviews varied significantly between the four local authorities in the study. In the local authority which had a particularly well-organised system, 63 per cent of reviews were held at six-monthly intervals compared with rates ranging from 30 per cent to 13 per cent in the others. There were also large differences between the local authorities in the length of the intervals between reviews: the authority which had a high proportion of regular reviews had only 12 per cent of cases where at least one gap extended to a year or more, while this applied at the other extreme to nearly three-quarters (73%) of the cases in another of the authorities.

It may be, of course, that cases were reviewed as the occasion arose and that because these were not part of the framework of routine procedures with forms to be completed they were not recorded. Sinclair, for example, concluded that the major decisions in child care were taken outside the review process and that these processes did 'not play a vital part in developing and monitoring long-term plans for children in care'.[2] Our results lend some support to this conclusion since a third of the placements that we considered to be detrimental to the child (on our fourfold classification) were reviewed at regular six-monthly intervals and this proportion was similar to the frequency of reviews for the more positive evaluations. Outcomes were not significantly associated with the regularity with which placements were reviewed and action was not necessarily taken to deal with poor placements as a result of a review. Of course, a selective process may once again be at work inasmuch as the most difficult and fragile placements were the ones that were regularly reviewed whereas in the case of those that were thought to be progressing well it was not felt to be imperative that reviews were done on time.

Parents or other carers were recorded as having been present at six-monthly reviews in only 21 cases (12%), and the majority of these were in one local authority. Only nine children attended at least one review during their period home on trial (5%), and again most of them were in this one local authority. Thus, twice as many parents attended a review during home on trial as attended the meeting or conference held to make the decision for the placement, while a similar number of children were involved at both stages. But the extent of involvement of parents and children was very low on both occasions. Sinclair found a similar picture in her study of decision-making at reviews during 1981 and 1982.[3] It is likely that practice has changed in relation to the inclusion of parents and children in reviews since our study was undertaken. However, given that a quarter of the Protected children were still home on trial at the beginning of 1986, we might have expected a greater degree of parental and child involvement than was recorded.

The attendance of parents and children at conferences and reviews is clearly an important issue if their views are to be considered and if they are to feel involved in the progress of the placements. For example, Packman and her colleagues found at the six month follow-up of their cohort that the parents of children on compulsory orders 'continued to feel that matters had been taken out of their hands ... Many also felt impotent to influence social workers' plans for their child and a third ... expressed considerable anger at the nature (or sometimes the lack) of such plans'.[4] In our study, successful home on trial placements were significantly associated with parental attendance at six-monthly review meetings, although the number was small. We cannot, however, assume that parental attendance led to success. It may well be that social workers were more willing to include parents in reviews when placements were going well.

Discharging Orders

In 88 per of the cases at least one six-monthly review took place whilst the child was home on trial. However, the existence of reviews does not necessarily imply that regular consideration was given to whether or not an application should be made to the court for the discharge of the care order. Indeed, in a third of the cases that were reviewed there was no evidence that such a step was discussed. Among the cases where the discharge of the order was not considered there were no significant differences according to legal status, duration of the placement, or outcome. Yet the law is clear that the discharge of an order should be considered at every review. The Children and Young Persons Act, 1969, in section 27(4), directs that if a care order is in force, at the six-monthly review the local authority should 'consider in the course of the review whether to make an application for the discharge of the order'. The local authority is also legally required under sections 1 and 90 of the Child Care Act, 1980 to seek rehabilitation and to consider the discharge of a care order. Our findings on this matter are in line with those of the small in-house study of home on trial in Sheffield, previously mentioned, which also found that an application for the discharge of the order was not actively considered in over a third of the cases scrutinised.[5] Similarly, in the Children's Legal Centre study of reviews only eight out of 63 local authorities mentioned the consideration of the discharge of the order as one of the purposes of reviews.[6]

Nonetheless, discharge of the order or the rescission of a parental rights resolution was considered for 56 per cent of the cases, for most of them on more than one occasion. Yet although discharge was considered for a little over half of the Protected children, it materialised for only 31 per cent of them during our study period. We did not discover why such a disparity existed. Obviously, at times it would be because there were continuing concerns about the child. However, it is also likely that in the absence of a specific policy on the early discharge of orders, caution and the line of least resistance may have prevailed.

At the time of the study none of the four local authorities had precise written policies on the discharge of orders,[7] although at various times there had been attempts to ensure that they did not go on for too long. A number of reasons why orders might not be discharged were suggested by one local authority. Some parents and some older children did not wish the order to be discharged, particularly when they valued the relationship with the social worker. Staff in this local authority suggested that schools at times saw the discharge of an order as the social services department opting out and therefore applied pressure for the order to remain in force. The maintenance of a child's placement with a particular carer was also mentioned as a reason for orders remaining; for example where the custody of the child was in dispute between the parents. Finally, it was said that social workers might be disinclined to take the time to prepare reports for proceedings in court. During interviews, we found that on occasion an order was not discharged because the field worker wished to ensure that supervision could be maintained over other members of the family who were not on orders, although such a practice might not usually be made explicit. In one of our earlier studies we suggested that sometimes orders were kept in place to preserve children's eligibility for financial help.[8] In view of the low levels of payments actually made this could rarely have been a compelling reason for maintaining an order.

Even if the local authority did not choose to apply for the discharge of an order, the parent or child could do so. It was interesting to find that there were only five successful parental applications for the discharge of orders among the Protected group, and in two of these the care order was varied to a supervision order. All five applications were unopposed by the local authority. One parent also made an unsuccessful application. However, 23 parents had threatened to apply for the discharge of a care order as a way of securing the return of their child. As we have seen, local authorities tended to take such threats seriously and might well offer a home on trial placement in preference to dealing with the application in court. We had thought that parents might be less likely to threaten to make an application for the discharge of an order once the child was home. Whilst this turned out to be true in terms of actual applications, 20 parents contemplated applying during the home on trial period. Most took no further action, although four consulted a solicitor but did not proceed. In nine cases the same parents who had threatened legal action to get the child home also considered applying for the discharge of an order once the child was there but took matters no further.

The Child Abuse Register

The child abuse register, now known as the child protection register, is another important procedure for monitoring children's progress. In contrast to the pattern of statutory reviews, action on registration and de-registration was very similar in each of the four local authorities. Sixty-three (37%) of the Protected children were on the register whilst they were in care prior to going home on trial. By the time that they were placed at home their number had risen to 80 (46%). Only 55 (79%) of the 70 children who were subject to orders for abuse were on a register during their time home on trial. Twenty-two (40%) of the 55 children on orders for neglect were on a register as were three who were on orders on grounds other than abuse or neglect. Of the total of 80 children who were on a register, 32 (40%) had their names removed whilst they were home on trial (during the period of the research) but 41 (51%) did not. There were seven children for whom this information was unclear. The proportions of children de-registered during home on trial were similar for children subject to orders made on the grounds of abuse or neglect.

We checked to see whether registration related to the level of planning and monitoring that children received. Such a relationship did appear to exist, since 43 per cent of the children on a register had rehabilitation planned for them at the outset as compared with only 25 per cent of the unregistered children. However, it is somewhat surprising to find that in the case of as many as a fifth (21%) of the registered children no clear plan had been made within six months of the compulsory order; but this is still considerably lower than the 37 per cent of unregistered children for whom no plans had been made. The difference is statistically significant.

As might be expected, the frequency of reviews was also related to whether children were on an abuse or 'at risk' register. Thus, 43 per cent of the children who remained on a register during home on trial had reviews at six-monthly intervals compared with 28 per cent of those whose names were removed and 24 per cent of those who were never registered. Gaps of over a year between reviews occurred for half the children who had never been registered or who were de-registered, but for only a third of those who stayed on a register. Nonetheless, it is surprising that such long intervals could occur for children subject to organised child protection procedures.

* * *

Thus, our evidence suggested that the monitoring of home on trial placements was uneven, at least according to the written records. Informal reviews and evaluation may have filled the gap, but we do not know. In any case, the difficulties and risks associated with returning abused or neglected children would seem to demand formal processes of review and assessment that involve a number of people, not least the parents and children. Over and above that the systematic and comprehensive monitoring of home on trial placements provides a basis for sharing experience and learning from what has been done. It is encouraging to see that the new regulations and the accompanying guidance place considerable emphasis upon monitoring; but that emphasis, and the associated legal requirements, remain to be translated into practice if they are to achieve the improvements that are intended. However, the evidence from this and other studies of the extent to which statutory six-monthly reviews are not conducted, or conducted late, indicate that such monitoring procedures themselves need to be monitored.

In this respect our findings have a particular value since they are the only reasonably large-scale account of the state of affairs before the implementation of the Charge and Control regulations in 1989. They offer, therefore, a basis for the evaluation of the effects of such regulations, in this case in respect to the fulfilment of the monitoring requirements.

Notes and references

1. See Sinclair (1984), *op. cit.*, for example.
2. *Ibid*, para. 3; p. 151.
3. *Ibid.*
4. Packman (1986), *op. cit*; p. 181.
5. Cooper, 1982, *op. cit.*
6. Children's Legal Centre, *It's My Life, Not Theirs*, 1984.
7. For a more up-to-date review of local authorities' written child care policies see, Department of Health, Social Services Inspectorate, *Child Care Policy: Putting it in Writing. A Review of English Local Authorities' Child Care Policy Statements*, HMSO, 1990.
8. E. Farmer and R. A. Parker, *A Study of the Discharge of Care Orders*, Department of Social Administration, University of Bristol, 1985.

CHAPTER 11

How the Home on Trial
Placements Ended

The Outcomes at the End of the Follow-up

As we have noted, the outcomes of the home on trial placements were recorded whenever they occurred after 31st March, 1984 up to a maximum period of two years from that date. An outcome refers either to a change of legal status while the child was home on trial (for example if the care order was discharged) or to a move out of the original home on trial household. By the end of the follow-up period a quarter of the Protected children were still in the original home on trial placement. Almost another third had had their care order discharged. The care orders had expired for just 7 per cent as they reached the age of eighteen whilst still at home. Altogether 38 per cent of the placements had broken down and these children were either living in a different household whilst retaining their home on trial status or they had moved back into the main care system or into custody. The home on trial had not achieved 'permanence' for these children although it could have served to re-establish their contacts with their families. The table which follows gives the outcomes.

Table 20. The Situation by the End of the Follow-up Period (31.3.86) for Home on Trial Placements
(There was no information on the outcome in 5 cases)

	%
The original home on trial placement was continuing	25
The care order had been discharged whilst the child was living at home on trial	30
The care order had expired whilst the child was living at home on trial	7
The home on trial placement had broken down	38
	100
	N = 167

The 63 placements which broke down did so for a variety of reasons. We recorded the principal reason why they ended, but in some cases (33 in all) a second reason was also important. In table 21 therefore, we have added together all the reasons in order to give a better idea of the kinds of factors, whether singly or together, that led to the breakdowns.

Table 21. The Principal and Secondary Reasons for the Termination of the Home Trial Placements
(The categories are not exclusive)

	%
Abuse or neglect	13
Risk of abuse or neglect	8
Breakdown of relationships with the child	25
Child's request or decision to leave	15
Break-up of the household	13
Carer ill or imprisoned	8
Child's behaviour (for example, offending or being beyond control)	13
Other	5
	100
	N = 96

In all, three-fifths (61%) of the reasons for the placements being discontinued were said to be difficulties of one sort or another in the relationships between the adults in the household and the child. Within this category the most common reason was a general deterioration in relationships (25%) followed by the child taking the initiative to leave (15%). Abuse or neglect (or the risk of one or the other) constituted about a fifth (21%) of all reasons given for the terminations.

Another fifth (21%) of the reasons for the placements breaking down were related to circumstances in which the parent figures were no longer in a position to look after the child, either because their own relationship had disintegrated, sometimes leading to homelessness, or because of illness or imprisonment. This again points to the fragility of some of the households to which children return, and is in contrast to those of the Disaffected group of children where, as we shall see later, household break-up was rarely a reason for a home on trial ending. Finally, a small proportion (13%) of the reasons for the placements of the Protected group ending were attributable to the child's behaviour; that is, to offending or to other behaviour which the parent figures could not control.

It was interesting to find that although almost a quarter of the children attended school fitfully or not at all, poor school attendance was never recorded as the main reason for a home on trial ending and was given as a secondary reason in just two cases. Presumably, school attendance is generally not considered an important enough issue to merit the dissolution of a home on trial placement.

It is important to note that in spite of the powers held by local authorities to remove children from home on trial placements, social services department were not the main actors in terminating placements. The major initiative was taken by parents or children, accounting for three-fifths of all endings. Only a third of the terminations were initiated by social services departments.

The Fortunes of the Children whose Placements Broke Down

A variety of subsequent moves were made by the 63 children whose home on trial broke down. Thirty-five of them (55%) were placed in substitute care but another 22 (35%) moved directly to another household whilst still retaining their home on trial status. They revealed an interesting phenomenon which national statistics obscure. When children are recorded as being home on trial they may not be settled with one family but may be subject to a number of moves among the parents, extended family and friends. Finally, six children moved either into a flat or lodgings or into custody.

Table 22. The Child's Accommodation After the Original Home on Trial Placement Terminated

	%
Home on trial with other carers	35
Residential care	30
Foster care	25
Other	10
	100
	N = 63

Of the 35 children who moved back into substitute care when their home on trial placement ended, only seven returned to exactly the same care placement in which they had lived before: three to the same foster parents and four to the same residential home. Thus, it was rarely possible to shield children from having to adjust to yet another major change. Furthermore, the records showed that social workers intended that 10 of these children should return home on trial once more and that the other 25 should be found a permanent placement in the care system.

We have seen that 22 children started their placement in one household and then moved on to another that was still classified as home on trial. One child moved to both parents from grandparents, nine moved to a single parent (usually a move from one parent to the other), four went to grandparents, two to other relatives and six to friends. Over three-quarters of these rearrangements were made by the children or the families themselves without the involvement of the social services department except inasmuch as they raised no objections.

For eight children the new home on trial placement was continuing at the end of the follow-up period. For the other 14 the new home on trial broke down, often after quite a short period: eight lasted for less than six months. Some of these children moved on to a third or even a fourth consecutive home on trial placement.

Whereas only nine of the original home on trial placements were with relatives seven more occurred as a result of these subsequent changes, three of which with grandparents were converted in due course into foster placements that attracted a boarding-out allowance. However, it was by no means clear how a decision was made as to whether a placement with relatives would be left to stand as a home on trial or be approved as a foster placement. In none of these home on trial placements had compulsory care occurred because of shortcomings in the care offered by the relatives, so the notion of the placement as a trial did not appear to apply.

The whole question of the status of relatives who look after children in care remains somewhat ambiguous, even though it often appears to be a successful arrangement. Although most of those who have used the custodianship provisions have been relatives[1] the very small number of such orders (accompanied by the payment of custodianship allowances) has done little to clarify the position. Likewise, the Charge and Control regulations left the matter open to the discretion of the local authority.[2]

We suspect that some of the longstanding ambiguity that surrounds the question of how much assistance (particularly financial assistance) parents should receive also extends to relatives, especially close relatives, who have been expected to accept a measure of responsibility for their grandchildren, their brothers and sisters or their nephews and nieces that lies somewhere between what is expected of a parent and what is expected of an unrelated foster parent.

The Duration of the Placements

Having looked in some detail at the placements which broke down it is important to re-emphasise that not all of them would necessarily be considered to have been detrimental to the child. On the other hand, some of those which were continuing at the end of our review period in 1986 would doubtless break down later. An important factor to be borne in mind in interpreting these data is how long the placements had lasted, either up to the point of their breakdown, to the discharge or expiry of the order or (for those which were continuing) by the end of March, 1986.

Since our sample was drawn from children who were home on trial on 31st March, 1984, they would already have been with their families or relatives for varying periods by that date. As we have explained, outcomes were recorded at any time up to the 31st March, 1986. Thus, placement durations were not uniform.[3] Given this proviso, we found that only 13 per cent of the placements had lasted less than a year, nearly half had lasted between one and three years and nearly 40 per cent had continued for over three years. The shortest placement survived only a month and the longest twelve and a half years. The average duration was 38 months. The following table gives the details.

Table 23. The Duration of Home on Trial Placements

	%
Less than 6 months	6
6 months, less than 1 year	7
1 year, less than 2 years	21
2 years, less than 3 years	27
3 years, less than 6 years	26
6 years or more	13
	100

A small study of home on trial placements in Leicestershire, carried out by Sinclair in 1986, also showed that children tended to remain in these placements for several years.[4] A very similar proportion of the children in her study were in home on trial placements for over two years (64%) as in our study (66%).

Even when placements broke down they frequently did so, as we have seen, after quite prolonged periods. Thus, of the 63 placement breakdowns only a quarter occurred within the first year home, whilst nearly two-fifths (37%) happened after more than two years. (This pattern held true no matter what the reason for the breakdown; for example whether it was because of family disintegration, abuse, or the child's decision to leave). This is similar to the timing of foster home breakdowns reported in the Berridge and Cleaver study, 40 per cent of which occurred after over two years in long-term foster placements.[5]

Social services departments appeared to exercise considerable caution about applying for the discharge of care orders. Care orders were discharged in respect of 51 children during out two-year follow-up period, but half of them occurred after three or more years home on trial.[6] Only just over a quarter (27%) were discharged within the first two years. The mean duration of home on trial placements by the time that care orders were discharged was three and a half years and the maximum just over nine years.

The caution that these figures suggest may not have been entirely misplaced in view of the long time before some of the breakdowns occurred. However, it does raise questions about the function of home on trial and whether it is in fact really used as a 'trial period', since it might be supposed that a trial would be time-limited and have the ending of the trial as the reward for success. It might be more appropriate in cases where prolonged supervision is considered to be necessary to vary the care order to a supervision order. This was rarely done; there were only five examples among all the Protected cases.

*   *   *

Given the theoretical rationale for home on trial placements it might be expected that either they were judged to have been successful in a relatively short time (say by two years) and the care order discharged, or shown to be unsatisfactory and the child removed and placed elsewhere. The reality, as we have seen, is much more complicated for several reasons.

First, the 'trial' is not necessarily the trial of a fixed set of arrangements. A satisfactory placement may become unsatisfactory as a result of changes in the household and *vice versa*. Secondly, little may change after the placement has been made and little new information come to light that indicates one way or another how the trial should be ended. This is particularly so if the placement was dubious or only marginally acceptable when it was made. Thirdly, there is a strong reluctance on the part of social workers to expose a child to yet further disruption unless removal is considered to be imperative. Fourthly, there are also strong policy pressures in favour of the restoration of children to their families wherever possible: this may lower the standard of acceptable parental care. If all the procedures now required by the regulations before a placement is made are fully implemented that standard may be raised and fewer children then returned home. Finally, the pattern of power in home on trial placements does not necessarily reflect the pattern of authority. Both children and parents are capable of exercising independent power (although they may not always realise it) and present social services departments with *faits accomplis*. We turn to consider some of these issues more fully in the next chapter.

Notes and references

1. Emma Bullard and Ellen Malos, *Custodianship: Caring for Other People's Children*, HMSO (forthcoming).
2. Department of Health, *Handbook of Guidance: Charge and Control Placements, op. cit.*, para. 4b. The regulations apply to relatives (or friends) if 'the degree of delegated responsibility is such that Boarding-Out Regulations do not apply'. But note that the latest proposals for revisions to bring the regulations in line with the Children Act, 1989, exclude carers in this category, instead making them subject to the foster care regulations.

3. This sampling method may have meant that longer placements were somewhat over-represented, since some short placements would not be included. The following table shows the dates at which the home on trial placements started.

The Year the Home on Trial Began for the Protected Children

	No.	*%*
1972–1978	22	13
1979–1980	20	11
1981–1982	55	32
1983–1984	75	44
	172	100

4. Leicestershire Social Services Department, *Children Home on Trial in Leicestershire*, Research Section, 1987.
5. Berridge and Cleaver, *op. cit.*
6. Differences were evident here between the four local authorities. Whilst in two of them two-thirds or more of orders were discharged after three or more years home on trial, in the other two authorities only about a third of orders were discharged after this period, the remainder having been discharged earlier.

CHAPTER 12

Some Issues for Social Work Practice
with Protected Children
Home on Trial
and their Families

Planning and Assessment

Our study of the home on trial placements of Protected children raises important issues for social work practice. By definition, procedures had been invoked which transferred parental responsibility from the parents to the local authority. However, as we have seen, in relation to planning for the future this responsibility was exercised more vigorously on behalf of some children than others. Thus, children subject to child protection registration and children under two were most likely to have plans made at the outset for their future and to be restored early. This raises the question of whether plans could also be made at the outset for more of the children who have been subjected to neglect or who have experienced family breakdown.

Even so, most of the plans which were made could more accurately be called intentions, since they usually indicated a hope or expectation that the child would be restored in the future rather than a plan of action. What was generally missing from the files was a specification of the circumstances that would enable a child to be placed home on trial; of the tasks required (of the parent figures and social worker) to realise these circumstances, and a time scale for their achievement.

In the absence of clearly defined goals for progress towards restoration, children tended to linger in substitute care and then the deciding factors in their eventual returns were likely to revolve around whether they or their parents exerted pressure to be reunited, or whether substitute care arrangements had broken down.[1] Greater specificity about what is required to restore children home; joint agreement with parent figures about the assignment of tasks, and commitment to a time scale would be beneficial in working towards making home on trial placements. It would also ensure that parent figures knew what was expected of them in order to secure their child's return. Certainly, the Oregon Project in the USA has demonstrated that a concentrated focus on the family which includes goal-setting and contracting with parents can help to get children home.[2]

This is not to suggest that preparation for restoration will always proceed smoothly, nor that the decision about the suitability of return for a child will be easy to make, particularly since, as we have seen, the children and parent figures often experience changes in their situations whilst they are separated. Indeed, in view of these changes it is important to think of home on trial as a 'new placement' and assess it accordingly, something which the regulations serve to emphasise.[3] One crucial question that needs to be answered before a home on trial placement is made is who is in the household to which the child will go? We often found this difficult to determine from the files. It was frequently necessary to go back to the court reports and other items in order to obtain this information. It might be useful if these data were readily available on file: this would facilitate the kind of scrutiny (for example involving police checks on the adult members) that the regulations now require. We found that new cohabitees could join the household with little investigation of their background and role in the family. Case notes and reviews frequently reserved their comments for the relationship between the child and the main parent figure—usually the mother. As we have seen the whole network of relationships is important, including those involving the other children in the household.

The need for a thorough assessment will be just as great in the case of children whose return home is precipitated by outside pressures. Fostering and adoption placements are considered by a panel; something similar would be useful in the case of home on trial placements.[4] Our findings suggest that the more disrupted and the longer the period in care before the child goes home on trial, the greater the difficulties are likely to be. These factors, together with information about changes in the membership of the household, could provide useful indicators of the need for special support thereafter.

Responsibilities, Expectations and Conditions

We do not know how often a clear explanation of the respective responsibilities of the parties was given to the parent figures at the start of the home on trial placements. The legal situation in which the local authority retains parental powers and responsibilities, whilst handing to the parents the day-to-day care of their children, is complex and may be hard for the parents to grasp. We do know, however, that two of the local authorities required parents to sign a home on trial undertaking when the child went home. One of these agreement forms spelled out the fact that the local authority retained 'parental rights and powers' and the other explained that the child remained in the care of the local authority. Both stated that the child could be removed at any time, and that the parents undertook to allow the local authority's officers to see the child as necessary. On one of the forms parents agreed to have the child medically examined when the local authority required. Both enjoined the families to inform the local authority if they moved and one, as we have seen, added that the family was responsible for maintaining the child financially[5] and for ensuring regular school attendance.

Now that the regulations prohibit a home on trial placement being made until an agreement has been drawn up that covers all the points set out in the schedule to those regulations,[6] many of these issues should be clarified. The regulations also require that agreements are reconsidered and, if necessary, revised in light of the six-monthly reviews. Nonetheless, much is left for the local authorities to specify, in particular the precise responsibilities that those with day-to-day care of the child are expected to exercise and what remains the local authority's responsibility. Doubtless case law will gradually develop but it is obviously necessary for local authorities to adopt clear policies so that social workers, parents and children know where they stand.

However, clarification of the responsibilities associated with the status of home on trial is only a beginning. In general the files yielded surprisingly little information about what was expected to happen during the placement; about what would be needed for an order to be discharged or, alternatively, on what basis approval for the home on trial might be withdrawn and the child removed. This lack of specificity about expectations relating to return home on trial and the discharge of the order was reflected in the sparing use of formalised conditions for the child's return. Only one in five of the Protected cases was subject to such conditions, which normally related to the restriction of access to the child by a particular adult (usually an abusing parent); to the necessity for regular school or day nursery attendance, or to the acceptance of a service or treatment. The conditions that a child should have regular medical checks was rarely used. Where conditions were set, however, enforcement during home on trial was partial or ineffective in about half the cases. This emphasises an area of difficulty with the regulations; namely, the enforcement of the agreements where the only ultimate sanction is the removal of the child.

It was noteworthy that those placements in the study in which the conditions set for the child's return had been successfully applied were significantly likely to have positive outcomes. However, successful enforcement was typically associated either with parental co-operation, purposeful social work, or both.

A cautionary note should be sounded on the subject of conditions. The imposition of conditions which are not enforced will create difficulties about the basis of the home on trial placement. It is obviously important that only those conditions are set which the social worker has the intention and means of enforcing. There was an occasion when a social worker berated a family for not informing him of their move of house, apparently unaware that he had himself failed to act on another condition for home on trial, which was to make arrangements for regular medical checks. There were also examples of unrealistic conditions being set. For example, a wardship court imposed a curfew on the mother's boyfriend that restricted the hours he could visit the home. This was a condition that the social services department had no means of enforcing.

Written agreements that specified the progress which was expected once the child went home were also rare. There was evidence of the use of such contracts in only one in ten of the Protected cases. There was no significant variation between the local authorities in their use, although in one of them the director had circulated a memorandum at the end of 1985 requesting the use of contracts for all child abuse cases. The skilled use of such written agreements[7] (which are now mandatory) during home on trial could encourage a clarity of purpose as well as indicate the respective tasks of all parties. The parent would know what was expected and the social worker's attention would be kept focused on the kind of help that was needed to ensure that the arrangement worked. The Tyra Henry report[8] considered that such an agreement would have been helpful in her case, both in specifying that the placement was with the grandmother and in ensuring that she received adequate help with her financial and housing problems.

Power and Authority

This discussion of the need for clarity of expectations is based on the assumption that the local authority is in a strong position to set the agenda for home on trial. In reality this is not always the case. When a department has been able to retain the initiative for making the home on trial placement, then the worker is likely to be in a position to set the ground rules and retain the balance of power. However, for that group of children who go home on trial principally because of outside pressures, the initiative moves away from the local authority into the hands of the child and family who may themselves have determined if and when the return should occur. These situations include placements that are *faits accomplis*, where the child or parents force the hand of the local authority, for example by the child running home or being taken away from substitute care by the parents. Another situation arises with 'last resort' placements which are made because the substitute care system has failed to contain the child; for example when he or she had proved impossible to cope with, either because of difficult behaviour or because of insistence on rejoining the family. In such 'last resort' placements, and in those where the social services department is anxious to return a child home on trial but where parental motivation for reunion is weak or inconsistent, the local authority may actually be beholden to the family for taking the child. If local authorities are indebted to families for receiving their children home, or have given up their authority in the face of a challenge to it, then the return of the child is not primarily in the local authority's gift. This involves a crucial shift in the balance of power. The delicate nature of this balance and the assumptions behind it were revealed in one instance of a family who, after having two of their children home on trial for over a year, requested that one of them be returned permanently to substitute care. The local authority which had assumed that the child's stay at home was at their determination, discovered that it was not.

A social worker's ability to set standards and ensure that they are maintained during home on trial ultimately depends upon having some bargaining counters, either to reward or to penalise. Discharge of the care order could in theory be offered as a reward for a specified degree of progress, but as far as we could see this was rarely done. Such practice was evident in only nine per cent of the Protected cases. This may be because social workers do not wish to proceed in this way, fearing that the consequence would be to precipitate discharge. Alternatively, the appeal of the discharge of the order as a reward may not be very great. Some parents may not consider that its existence matters once their child is home, although in her study of children home on trial Thoburn found more resentment among families about undischarged orders than the social workers thought.[9] Some parents and older children may also resist the order being discharged either because they see it as a support or because, in the case of the parent of a difficult teenager, they want it available as an employable threat.[10]

As we have said before, the only real sanction that can be invoked during home on trial is the removal of the child, and it is on this that, in the last analysis, the social worker's power is based. Yet in practice removal is often neither desirable nor even feasible, given the extent of disruption that children have already experienced and the other options that are available. Thus, unless the child has been returned home on trial to a situation where the fear of removal represents a real sanction—that is one which could be invoked and where a suitable alternative care placement could be found—then the exercise of the social worker's responsibilities during home on trial can rest only on persuasion.

However, the sanction of removal may provide an effective basis for the social worker's authority even though, in reality, it would not be used. That is because the parents or other carers may believe that it would be employed if they failed to conform to what was (or what they thought was) expected of them. Certainly, in our interviews with parents we found some who were aware that the social services department would be loath to move the child; but there were others who were fearful that the slightest transgression on their part would see their child removed. Thus, although it is true that under most circumstances in their interactions with social workers the parents' power is considerable not all of them realise the potential strength of their position. Indeed, in many other aspects of their dealings with officialdom they will have had their sense of powerlessness reinforced; not least, of course, in their experience of having their child compulsorily removed in the first place.

It is difficult to say how far social workers are conscious of the delicate balance of power that may exist and, more particularly, whether they are conscious of how it is perceived by the parents or parent figures. In some cases they may in fact engage in a game of bluff, knowing that the parents are desperately anxious to retain the child whilst also knowing that they would only recommend removal as a last resort. The circumstances may be even more complicated than that if one of the carers (usually the birth parent) is fearful that the child will be taken away whilst the other (usually a cohabitee or step-parent) is largely indifferent to what might happen or would actually welcome the child's departure.

It can be seen, therefore, that a social worker will have maximum leverage when returning a young abused child to parents who are highly motivated to get the child back and worried lest removal occur again. The situation will be very different when a child who has been in care for several years is returned home on trial to somewhat reluctant parents because, for example, the foster placement has broken down. The parents are likely to be aware of the lack of an alternative, especially if the child's behaviour is very disruptive and difficult to manage. The social worker will not then be in a position to assert rigorous conditions. Indeed, in 24 cases (14%) in the Protected group of children the worker had serious difficulties in gaining access to the child and family during home on trial. These children had significantly poor home on trial placements. This raises real questions about how the responsibilities of the authority can be adequately discharged when the social worker's leverage, or even access, is so problematic.[11]

The reluctance of social services departments to invoke the sanction of removal lies close to the heart of this dilemma. As has been shown, departments had stepped in to end only a third of the terminated placements, involving 20 children. In addition, nearly half of the home on trial placements which in our view were detrimental for the child had lasted for over two years.[12] A great deal of effort was put into supporting some placements and attempts were made to absorb or smooth over further incidents of concern in preference to removing the child.

Thus, renewed abuse and neglect might be tolerated if the social worker believed that the family was generally co-operative. Poor attendance at school was also very likely to be allowed, since this was regarded overtly on case files as less important than adequate family relationships. Some children in the study had experienced a series of incidents of abuse or neglect, sometimes over long periods, before compulsory care was initiated, often by means of a place of safety order. It may be that in some situations any such reluctance to remove children into compulsory care in the first place[13] is exceeded by the reluctance to remove them once they have been returned on a home on trial placement. Thus, the considerations which lead to the removal of a child into compulsory care may be different from those which later determine whether he or she should be removed from home on trial.

It may be useful to illustrate this issue by an example of a placement in the study which was not terminated. Sharon was neglected and twice sustained abuse involving facial bruising and black eyes before a care order was made when she was three. She was quickly returned to her mother but removed eighteen months later on the recommendation of the NSPCC because of further facial bruising. A subsequent case conference revealed that some participants thought that Sharon should never go back home, whilst social services personnel were committed to her return. As a result, she was placed home on trial again and by our follow-up date had remained there for over six years. However during that time, as recorded in the file, she was injured again and together with the other children was left alone in the house. Sharon failed to gain weight, remained on the third centile and was scapegoated by her mother who expected her to look after the younger children. A psychiatric report on the mother offered the comment that the home was 'an unstable and unsuitable environment' for the children.

How can we best understand the apparent reluctance to remove some children from unsatisfactory placements home on trial? It may be that social workers sometimes feel that living in such a home is better for children than not being home at all; and, of course, this may be true. It may also be that the desire to retain children at home, especially in the light of previous disruptions and concern about their future if in care, may lead to some social workers developing a high threshold of tolerance for essentially unsatisfactory states of affairs. Home on trial, far from being regarded as a trial, may rather be seen as a thinly disguised permanent arrangement. However, there may be other reasons. The very fact of a child's return home on trial is tantamount to an official endorsement of the placement. It may then be difficult to decide to withdraw that endorsement, particularly in the absence of a major crisis such as serious abuse to the child. Continuing low standards of care may not be seen as a sufficient reason for taking such a step.

The issues for social services departments are complex and require fine judgement. The context of such judgements is that local authorities use different standards in relation to home on trial placements than they apply to foster or residential care. Few, if any, local authorities would accept a rate of abuse or neglect of one in four or, indeed, a similar rate of poor attendance at school in these settings. It is also clear that local authorities approve home on trial households that would not pass the scrutiny applied to foster families. These would include, for example, mothers who work as prostitutes, families who, by different devices, block social workers' access to the children, and mentally ill parents. Likewise, relatives who had children placed with them home on trial, rather than being treated as foster parents, may be those whom it is considered would not meet the standards expected by a fostering panel.

Standards

Thus, the reality is that the local authority *in loco parentis* accepts situations for children home on trial which many in the community would condemn. It will be recalled that the panel exercise that we undertook using case studies from the sample underlined this. We found that, in general, 'insiders' (that is, social workers and team leaders) evaluated home on trials more positively than 'outsiders' (that is, those who were involved with children but more distant from everyday practice; for example, social work teachers, psychiatrists and other professionals) who rated the same placements in considerably more negative terms. Children who had been in care also tended to rate the placements more negatively, as did parents of children in care. A similar split was recorded at some case conferences when the police or NSPCC officers were quite opposed to placements which social services departments wished to make. The report on the inquiry into Malcolm Page's death made this point.[14] It suggested that when a worker is constantly exposed to a deprived population, standards may be adjusted downwards to an unacceptable level. It was considered that the views of others might then provide a useful corrective. However, it is not just a question of standards in relation to a deprived population but also a question of the lack of appropriate care resources and the damage and disruption shown by children's individual histories.

Clearly, there is no simple answer to the questions that such issues raise since in general, family of birth placements for these children cannot be expected to offer the standard of care of a carefully selected substitute family; yet children may nonetheless be well placed at home. One social work manager who took part in our evaluation exercise summed up something of this dilemma when he wrote:

> I fear that some of my 'positive' and 'adequate' judgements may be seen by some of my colleagues as too pragmatic and relative and not sufficiently directed towards the ideal; but in the real world, in my experience, children's interests are best served by balancing real life chances and risks. I suppose I am saying that the world must be accepted as it is and not as we would remake it using social worker skills and resources. An important benchmark for me is . . . whether they have allowed a feeling of 'belonging' to the natural family to persist for the child. If that is the case, then I think many other aberrations are acceptable.

It was interesting that in a small number of the protected cases (17) social workers seemed more confident in invoking the sanction of removal of the child. This was when they were doubtful about the viability of the home on trial in the first place but felt that it had to be tried. In these cases they were clear that in the event of its breaking down they would seek an alternative long-term placement. In most (12), but not all of these cases, this had been made clear to the parents. This suggests that social workers feel able to remove children from home on trial when they have made contingency plans for the permanent care of the children outside the family. It may be, therefore, that as the concept of permanence planning is taken up more fully, social workers will be willing to give home on trial their full support to try to ensure that if possible it will work, but also be ready to end it if it fails to meet a child's needs. At the moment, home on trial placements may at times be in danger of falling between these two stools and create yet another state in which the child is kept in unsatisfactory limbo.

We wondered whether social workers and parents viewed these placements, as the name implies, as a trial: and, if so, who or what was on trial?
Since most of these children were under 13 when they were placed at home
and the majority had been abused or neglected, or their parents had been
unable to care for them, it might be assumed that it was the parents rather
than the children who were on trial and that the essence of the trial
concerned their parenting capability and their ability to provide a suitable
home. However, in the case of children who had been removed from parents
and later placed with relatives, the nature of a trial would then be more
obscure, unless their ability to care (or to cope financially) was also
considered to be problematic.

It is surprising that until recently the term home on trial continued to be
used, for much of the evidence that we have reported indicates that, in
practice, home on trial placements were not viewed simply as a trial or as
a period of probation. In the case of the Protected group of children at least,
such placements more clearly resembled prolonged supervised care at home.

In view of the ambiguous status of home on trial and the dilemmas that
it poses, it was very encouraging to find that social workers who could
maintain a clear sense of purpose, together with a readiness to use their
authority (and to plan how it might be used) were able to make a difference
to the outcome of these placements. This often required the ability to view
the changes in fortunes of the families and children in a broad context whilst
at the same time maintaining a clear focus in the work that was done. There
were a number of factors which indicated purposeful social work and which
were significantly associated with successful home on trial placements. It has
been seen that decisive planning for the child's return got children home
quickly, and that return within a year was associated with success. Other
factors which were significantly associated with successful placements, and
which indicated purposeful social work were: that the social worker had
maintained the initiative for the child's return home on trial; that the case
was allocated throughout the placement; that a firm oversight was maintained of the child's progress; that the level of risk during placement was
clearly recorded for abused children; that parents were involved in six-
monthly reviews, and that conditions were set and enforced.

*   *   *

Changes in terminology often indicate a turning point in attitudes and
opinions. In a brief space of time home on trial placements began to be
known as charge and control, but this will shortly be overtaken by the
somewhat unspecific terminology 'accommodation with parents etc.' under

the Children Act, 1989. New emphases may emerge. The very fact that these placements are now subject to statutory regulation is a major step forward in their recognition as arrangements that call for careful preparation, supervision and monitoring; that they should be regarded as 'new' placements to be overseen with as much, if not more care than any others. Nevertheless, there remain inherent difficulties for social workers, especially in the case of the Protected children. They are difficulties that revolve around the issue of control. Our evidence suggests that it is possible for social workers to perform the balancing act that is called for; but for that to happen great clarity of purpose is necessary, a purpose that has to be equally clear from the outset to the parents, relatives and children if they are of an age to appreciate it. Otherwise the deep-seated ambiguity of these placements will remain despite the regulations and will cause unnecessary misunderstanding, obfuscation, indecision and, potentially, harm to the child.

Notes and references

1. It is likely that once children are in care different considerations are applied to their return than were applied to the issue of their removal. A study carried out in Lambeth showed that whilst 47 per cent of social workers thought an additional service might have prevented admission to care, six months later only 27 per cent of them thought an extra service might rehabilitate a child. L. Simpson, *What Happens to Children in Care? A Report on Children in Care in Lambeth*, Lambeth Social Services Department, 1981. Similarly Vernon and Fruin's study (1986, *op. cit.*) showed that once children were in care the focus of social workers shifted to considerations about the stability of care placements.
2. V. Pike, 'Permanency Planning for Foster Children: the Oregon Project' in *Children Today*, 5(6), 1976, and J. Lahti, 'A Follow-up Study of Foster Children in Permanent Placements', in *Social Service Review*, 56(4), 1982.
3. See, *Handbook of Guidance: Charge and Control Placements*, *op.* cit. For instance, 'the fact that the child is to be placed with an adult known to the child and the agency does not make proper preparations for the placement less necessary' (para. 20). And again, 'charge and control should be regarded as a major change on which a case conference would expect to comment' (para. 29). See also, Department of Health, The Children Act, 1989, Consultation Paper no. 9, *Accommodation of Children with Parents etc. (Guidance and Regulations)*, 1990.

4. It was the intention of an unsuccessful private members' bill introduced by Dennis Walters that decisions about home on trial placements should be made by the juvenile court. *Children and Young Persons (Amendment) Bill*, 1985.

5. There were a few cases where parents tried to elicit financial support during home on trial on the grounds that the children were still the responsibility of the social services department. A team leader described one such situation thus:

> We've had great difficulty in actually explaining to one woman what we meant by home on trial. She took the view that if the children went home on trial we should be paying her, we're responsible for the children, they're in our care. 'Why aren't you supporting them?' She was broke and she couldn't afford to feed them—we were their parents.

6. *The Accommodation of Children (Charge and Control) Regulations*, 1988, *op. cit.* and *Accommodation of Children with Parents etc*, 1990, *op. cit.*

7. See J. Aldgate (ed.), *Using Written Agreements with Children and Families*, Family Rights Group, 1989. The Family Rights Group has also produced a useful model form of written agreement.

8. *Whose Child? op. cit.*

9. Thoburn (1980), *op. cit.*

10. See, for example, the evidence in Farmer and Parker, 1985, *op. cit.*

11. The issue of unworkable care orders is also briefly addressed in the report by Farmer and Parker, *ibid.*

12. See also Lynch and Roberts, *op. cit.* The authors, in their study of abused children, felt concern about the poor quality of life of 29 of the 42 children.

13. Dingwall, Eekelaar and Murray, *op. cit.* The authors argue that in a liberal democratic society which values family privacy and minimal state intrusion, state agencies need compelling evidence to instigate care proceedings.

14. *Malcolm Page*, a report by the panel appointed by the Essex Area Review Committee, Essex County Council, 1981.

PART III

The Disaffected Children
Home on Trial

CHAPTER 13

Continuities

Introduction

In the previous section we looked at what had happened to a group of children who had been committed to care because of the risk or difficulty of their remaining at home but who were subsequently allowed to go home on trial. We turn now to consider the second group of children in our study; namely, those who were originally committed to care on the grounds that their behaviour gave cause for concern. We have explained why we decided to treat these two groups separately and why we refer to this second group of 149 youngsters, 70 per cent of whom were boys, as the 'Disaffected'.

The two groups—the Protected and the Disaffected—stand in such marked contrast to each other that one questions whether they should continue to be treated as the same administrative or legal category. Nonetheless, the regulations[1] make no distinction, possibly because the introduction of the 1989 Children Act is expected to reduce the number of young offenders and non-attenders at school who are committed to care. Henceforth, neither problem will, in itself, warrant such a committal unless the child 'is suffering, or is likely to suffer, significant harm' and unless that harm is attributable to a lack of the care that a reasonable parent might be expected to give.[2]

Even so, children will continue to be committed to care where the principal problem is considered to be the child's behaviour, albeit that that now has to be judged to be attributable to shortcomings in the care provided by the parents. However, children who are considered to be 'beyond parental control' remain an exception to this requirement (although their committal will be equally dependent upon proof of 'harm to the child'). This may actually encourage a greater use of that ground than in the past, although parents themselves will no longer be able to apply to the court for such an order.[3] Certainly, if social workers and others are reluctant to place the blame for a youngster's difficult behaviour on their parents, or if the evidence for that connection is dubious, they may well resort more often than before to applications for care orders on the ground that the child is beyond parental control.

Thus, the new regulations continue to cover some home placements which are similar to those experienced by the Disaffected group of children in this study. In light of our findings, however, we foresee difficulties in their application for at least three reasons.

First, as we pointed out in part I, nine out of ten of the children in the Disaffected group were 13 years old or more when they went home on trial and nearly two-fifths of them were 16 or 17. Only six were under 11. They were, therefore, adolescents, many of whom would in any case normally be leading lives which were at least partly beyond their parents' control. The awkward balance of power between social workers and parents that we discussed in relation to the Protected children is liable, therefore, to be further complicated in the Disaffected group by the independent actions of the young people.

Secondly, it is likely to be difficult (or inappropriate) for social workers to meet all the requirements of the regulations with respect to the selection of placements and their termination. Far from applying a stringent assessment it was not unusual for the social workers in our study to have appeared to have breathed a sigh of relief when the parents agreed to resume the day-to-day care of their Disaffected offspring. Similarly, they often appeared thankful if the arrangement for them to be at home could be kept going and problems ridden out without a fresh placement having to be found.

Thirdly, in considering the relevance of the regulations it is important to bear in mind that 45 per cent of those in the Disaffected group had been committed to care for offending; 36 per cent for persistent non-attendance at school and the remainder because they were deemed to be beyond their parents' control or because their behaviour placed them in 'moral danger'. Once home on trial, as we shall see, much of this worrisome behaviour recurred. Little seemed to have changed and, at least in comparison with the Protected group, this applied as much to the families to which the children returned as it did to the children's behaviour. Let us look at these two factors in rather more detail. Both of them, in their different ways, illustrate important continuities.

The Families to which the Children Returned

We have seen already that only a quarter of the Protected group of children went back to exactly the same household that they had left. By contrast two-fifths of the Disaffected category returned to an identical household. Table 24 sets out the changes in household composition that had taken place in the two groups. Whereas 52 per cent of the children in the Protected category found at least one different parent figure when they arrived home, this applied to only 28 per cent of the Disaffected group.

Table 24. Changes in the Composition of the Household to which the Children went Home on Trial (Excluding those who never left home and those where there was insufficient information)

	The Disaffected %	The Protected %
The child returned to:		
Identical household	38	25
Change in carer(s) only	8	22
Changes in other adults only	7	4
Changes in other children only	22	18
Changes in carer(s) and children	14	23
Changes in carer(s) and other adults	2	2
Changes in other adults and children	5	1
Changes in carer(s), children and other adults	4	5
	100	100
	N = 130	N = 153

As far as changes in the household were concerned, the Disaffected group differed from the Protected group in another respect: there was a significant positive relationship between the length of time the child had been in care before going home on trial and changes in the household. This suggested that the changes which occurred whilst they were away were more likely to have been due to the passage of time (for example, as older brothers or sisters left) rather than to the collapse of partnerships and their replacement by others.

If, instead of overall changes in household composition one concentrates upon the carer(s) the picture is somewhat different, but the variation between the Disaffected group and the Protected group remains distinct. A much larger proportion (31 per cent by contrast to 17 per cent) of the children in the Disaffected group went home to both birth parents and a smaller proportion to a step-parent household (18 per cent as against 40 per cent). The greater stability of the families of the Disaffected group (at least in terms of their households) is further emphasised if one compares the composition of the families that the children left with the ones to which they returned. Of those who were removed from both parents 80 per cent returned to them, by contrast with only 54 per cent amongst the Protected cases. Similarly, 84 per cent of those who had left lone mothers returned to lone mothers, whereas this was the case for only 55 per cent of the Protected category.

Thus, although there was a considerable amount of dislocation in all the families in the study, it was less pronounced amongst those of the Disaffected group. This conclusion was reinforced when we looked at what was happening to the children's brothers and sisters. In the Disaffected group the children were usually (83%) the only child home on trial in the household. This was in marked contrast to the Protected group (46%). Indeed, there were only 10 instances (7%) where a child in the Disaffected group was placed home on trial together with one or more siblings: in the Protected group there were 75 (44%). In addition, it should be noted that in the Disaffected group, whether or not children were returned together with a brother or sister bore no significant relationship to whether or not the placement was successful. This was in sharp contrast to the Protected group as we have seen.

The Disaffected group rarely entered care with brothers or sisters although, like the Protected cases, they tended to come from larger families than are found in the general population, and there were plenty of examples where older brothers or sisters had been in care but were now over 18. Where the grounds for an order were neglect or abuse children tended to enter care as groups of brothers and sisters; where they had offended, failed to go to school or were considered to be beyond control the process was much more age-related, so that if different children in the same family came into care they did so at different times. They were then likely to be returned at various times.

The Children's Behaviour whilst Home on Trial

There were three forms of 'behaviour' that we were able to examine in some detail: offending, school attendance and pregnancy. Obviously there are many other aspects of a child's experience that one should explore in order to obtain a rounded picture of what was going on whilst they were at home. The justification for concentrating on these three areas lies in the fact that, as we have seen, of those in the Disaffected group 45 per cent had been committed to care because they had offended, 36 per cent because they had failed to attend school and 19 per cent because they were judged to be beyond the control of their parents or because their behaviour was deemed to place them in moral danger.

Whilst they were home on trial our Disaffected group had a much higher rate of offending than the Protected cases: 55 per cent as compared with 18 per cent. These proportions were based only on those who had reached the age of criminal responsibility.[4] Nonetheless, part of this difference in the prevalence of offending may have been because the average age of the young people in the Disaffected group was greater even within this group.

It is difficult to compare the high rate of offending by the Disaffected group whilst they were home on trial with the rate of offending by other children in care because data are so sparse. This is surprising given that at least 12 per cent of the children admitted to care in England and Wales in 1984 arrived specifically because they had committed an offence.[5] The lack of information about offending whilst in care is also surprising given the considerable attention that has been paid to monitoring rates of recidivism amongst juvenile offenders dealt with in other ways. This uneven interest probably reflects the division of responsibility between the Home Office and the Department of Health. The Home Office is responsible for overseeing most of the disposals used to deal with young offenders (for example, probation, detention centres and youth custody) whereas the Department of Health has carried a much less extensive responsibility, but one that includes answering for what happens to young offenders who are committed to local authority care. Furthermore, of course, the Home Office has a substantial and long-standing responsibility for dealing with crime in general. Crime and its treatment are, therefore, at the forefront of its administrative and political concerns. This is not true in the case of the Department of Health, where other preoccupations obtrude. The Home Office (often through the work of its research unit) has regarded information about recidivism as a useful contribution to the evaluation of its policies in a variety of areas. Indeed, just before responsibility for all children's services was transferred to the DHSS in the early 1970s, the Home Office undertook a study of re-offending rates amongst children placed home on trial who had been found guilty of an offence and made subject to a care order. A rate of 45 per cent was reported.[6] This result was used to support the view held by many magistrates at the time that care orders were an unsatisfactory replacement for approved school orders because they allowed the new social services departments a free hand to decide where a child should be placed.

There was particular concern that many young offenders were left at home or quickly returned there 'home on trial'.[7]

Almost certainly it was anxiety about the force of these criticisms that prompted the Social Work Service of the DHSS to commission a study of re-offending amongst children committed to care on offence grounds. It took the form of a national postal survey of all children committed to care in July 1975 for offending. Local social services departments returned question-naires on almost 500 children and recorded what happened over the next nine months. Almost half of the children were returned home at least once during this period. However, the length of their stay varied from a few days to the full duration of the study. Thirty-six per cent of the children were reported to have committed further offences over the nine month period.[8] A smaller study conducted at about the same time was based upon the records of one London court.[9] It showed that where children were sent home as a deliberate policy, the rate of re-offending over a year was 50 per cent, whereas for children who went home because of the lack of any other option it rose to 74 per cent. A lower offending rate amongst children placed at home purposefully as compared with those who went home for other reasons was not confirmed in our study.

If one looks at the prevalence of offending in the adolescent population as a whole the rates amongst the children in our Disaffected group whilst they were at home appear alarmingly high—68 per cent for the boys and 30 per cent for the girls, 57 per cent overall. For instance, the Cambridge Study in Delinquent Development which followed the lives of some 400 eight- and nine-year-old boys living in a working-class area of London from 1961 found that by the time they were 21 nearly a third (31%) were listed by the Criminal Records Office, although only 20 per cent had convictions as juveniles.[10] Power's later study in Tower Hamlets found an almost identical prevalence rate amongst boys up to the age of 17.[11] Various national studies, which included both boys and girls, have emerged with rates of between 14 and 18 per cent amongst the adolescent age group. However, self-reported offence rates are higher and it may be that because they were in care, more of the Disaffected group's offending came to public notice. That may have been even truer because they were home on trial rather than in another care setting where more control could be exercised over what came to light and how it was dealt with thereafter.

It also needs to be borne in mind that 70 per cent of the Disaffected group were boys, of whom about half had been committed to care *as* offenders. The rate of re-offending amongst this particular group whilst home on trial was 70 per cent, a proportion similar to the rates of reconviction amongst boys of this age group whatever the disposal. Furthermore, although on average the placements home of the Disaffected group were of a shorter duration than the Protected group, many of them lasted for fairly long periods (the mean was 20 months). Indeed, 70 per cent of those who offended had been at home for more than a year and 42 per cent for more than two. This may help to account for the fact that half of those who offended did so on more than one occasion; the overall rate of multiple offending amongst those who had reached the age of criminal responsibility was 40 per cent—all but one being boys.

At least two other factors might be considered to have inflated the rate of offending amongst the Disaffected group who went home on trial. The first is the fact that 13 per cent of them (20 cases) arrived there from detention centres or youth custody, albeit that they were still subject to care orders. However, their rate of re-offending (65%) was hardly different from that for the group as a whole. A second explanation for the high rate of offending is more telling. Not all the children and young people whom we classed as having offended were prosecuted. We took as 'an offence' anything that was so recorded; for example, events that led to a police caution or that were reported to the police but led to 'no further action' being taken. Not all other studies have adopted this broad definition. All in all, therefore, looked at comparatively the findings about offending whilst home on trial may not be as bad as they appear at first sight.

Nonetheless, there was a good deal of recorded offending, especially amongst the boys and amongst those of them who had been admitted to care on the grounds of their delinquency. For the Disaffected group at least we might have used this rate of re-offending as a criterion for judging the success of the placement; after all, these children were committed to care ostensibly to reduce the likelihood of further offending. However, of all those who re-offended whilst home on trial we classified nearly a third (29%) as having had 'positive' placements and a further half (51%) as 'adequate', the next most favourable of our original fourfold classification. Only three were placed in the most adverse 'detrimental' group. Of course, we had previously decided that offending or re-offending in itself should not be used to assess the success of these placements and we imagine that that would be the standpoint of many social workers as well (although not necessarily of probation officers or the police). Support for this view is provided by the fact that whereas there were 81 children in the Disaffected group who had offended at least once whilst at home, in only 22 instances (27%) was offending recorded as the principal reason for the placement breaking down. If we place alongside this the fact that in 17 of these 22 cases the youngsters were removed from home as a result of a court making a detention centre or youth custody order, then it becomes plain that social services departments did not independently initiate removal as a result of delinquent behaviour. Indeed, we found only two cases where this was clearly what happened. Somewhat more surprising is that when we looked at the secondary reasons for placements breaking down, offending was mentioned in only three further instances. The conclusion to be drawn from these data is that social services departments did not treat offending whilst home on trial as a problem that was severe enough to invoke the sanction of removal, even where the original grounds for committal to care were a child's delinquent behaviour. This may well reflect the fact that most of the offences would be classified as petty theft.

School attendance was poor or non-existent in the case of 48 (57%) of the 84 children in the Disaffected group who should have been at school whilst they were home on trial. Given that two-fifths of that group had originally been committed to care for not going to school this, like the rate of re-offending, might be taken as an objective index of the 'failure' of placements home on trial—certainly if the proper education of the child in care is to be taken seriously.[12] Leaving aside what actually happens at school, we know that most children in care who are placed in residential establishments do go to school regularly and, as a recent DHSS inspectors' report pointed out, this is often a considerable achievement on the part of the staff, although of course it is much easier to ensure attendance when education is provided on the premises.[13] We know virtually nothing about the rate of non-attendance amongst adolescents in foster homes, although Hazel's study of the adolescent fostering scheme in Kent implied (without giving figures) that good rates of attendance were achieved: 'foster parents collaborated closely to check truancy'.[14]

Of the 48 children whose attendance at school was irregular or non-existent there were 27 (56%) who were also known to have offended, so that although there was some overlap between the two problems it was far from complete, partly because the rate of poor school attendance amongst the girls (who offended less) was significantly higher than it was for the boys. We do not know why this should be, but it may be connected with pregnancy which, as we shall see, was quite common; or it may have reflected their use as childminders whilst at home.

When it came to our evaluation of the placements using our fourfold ranking, a quarter of the poor attenders were placed in the 'positive' group and another 58 per cent in the next most favourable category. Only eight per cent were classed as 'detrimental'. Although 52 per cent (25) of the placements where there were school attendance problems broke down, this is similar to the picture for the offenders and for the Disaffected group as a whole. However, there were only five cases where not attending school was given as the principal reason for the placement terminating. Furthermore, in only two further instances were school attendance problems given as a secondary reason. Thus, it seems that a child's failure to go to school regularly was rarely considered to be a leading reason for the premature ending of a placement home on trial, although in four out of the five cases where it was, the social services department had initiated the action.

In the Disaffected group 37 per cent of the children who were expected to attend school received some form of special education, either during or before their placement. This is a high proportion and it might have been expected that attendance at such schools would have been more regular than at the ordinary day schools. There was some confirmation of this since just over half (55%) of those in special schools attended regularly by comparison with only some two-fifths (37%) of the others. There was no significant age difference between the two groups. Although these data suggest that special education improved the attendance of the Disaffected group, they also expose in starker relief the particularly high rate of 63 per cent attending irregularly or not at all amongst those at home but not classed as having special educational needs. If the protection of the educational interests and opportunities of children in care is to be regarded as an important objective then, unfortunately, it appears that this may be at odds with policies for returning them home, at least for the Disaffected group.[15] However, various evidence suggests that 'education' is currently not a major goal of social work with such children. For example, the Suffolk cohort study undertaken by the Personal Social Services Research Unit at the University of Kent found that the social workers responsible for a group of nearly 100 new admissions to care did not once include 'the promotion of the child's intellectual development' amongst their first three practice objectives. In contrast, however, 'helping the child so that he or she may return to their parents' was the second most commonly stated objective (the first being 'the provision of short-term care').[16]

We do not know exactly why many of the children in the Disaffected group who were home on trial failed to attend school regularly. The fact that many had been regarded as 'troublesome' in one way or another may well have encouraged both social services departments and education authorities to turn a blind eye to their absenteeism as long as other things were reasonably settled. It should be noted that two-thirds of the school-aged children were placed home on trial at the tail end of compulsory schooling in their fifteenth year and that there were a few exceedingly difficult children whom no school was prepared to admit.

It must also be borne in mind that, strictly speaking, those who cared for youngsters when they were at home on trial were not legally responsible for seeing that they went to school, since parental rights and duties were still retained by the departments. Nonetheless, a certain ambiguity about responsibility for ensuring school attendance may have allowed it to deteriorate to an extent that would not have been acceptable had the child been in a residential home where a local authority's responsibility for what happens is unequivocal. It appears from the new regulations that it is now the parent or relative's responsibility to ensure school attendance, although the issue is not absolutely clear.

Finally, one must consider how far the disrupted childhoods of these children, and the numerous moves that many of them had experienced, had led to such poor educational experiences (and therefore achievement) that school had come to be associated with failure, humiliation and discord and thus something to be avoided at all costs. Unfortunately, we did not collect data on the number of different schools the children had attended; it would certainly be important to check this in any future study. However, committal to care had almost invariably involved a change of school (sometimes several changes) and return home usually necessitated another.

Nineteen (or 44%) of the teenage girls in our Disaffected group became pregnant whilst they were home on trial.[17] Four of them had miscarriages or abortions. One of the babies was taken into care during the study period. Eight of these 19 placements (42%) broke down but in only one case was the move the result of deliberate action on the part of a social services department.[18] Moreover, there were no occasions when the pregnancy or the birth were recorded as either the primary or secondary reason for the placement having collapsed.

It was notable that although there were 17 black or mixed parentage girls in the Disaffected group who were or became teenage during their placement at home, only one became pregnant. Pregnancy whilst home on trial was almost entirely limited to white girls.

We do not know how many teenage girls become pregnant whilst in care but in the country as a whole the fertility rate per 1000 females aged 15–19 (all live births) was 26.9 in 1984; that is, something less than three per cent.[19] The rate of pregnancy will be slightly different but nowhere as great as the rate amongst the girls in this study who were placed home on trial.

It is noteworthy that among the much smaller group of teenage girls in the Protected group only 5 (14%) became pregnant. This may exemplify the particular problems of social control amongst the Disaffected group. Ironically, pregnancy might be seen as a 'solution' to the problem of 'moral danger'; for example, by altering and improving the relationship between girls and their mothers as well as by imposing new constraints upon their freedom, constraints which then diminish the level of public concern about the 'moral dangers' to which they were exposed. Adolescent pregnancy and motherhood create new problems which are liable to redefine status as well as the notion of risk in ways that have no male counterpart.

Exercising Control

Whatever their precise consequences the scale of offending, poor attendance at school and pregnancy amongst the youngsters home on trial suggests that such placements are likely to weaken control over their behaviour or that of others with whom they choose or are obliged to associate. Parents or relatives tended to report that they felt helpless to influence what the young people did; social services departments seemed to be equally powerless. Social workers have virtually no sanctions that they can or are willing to invoke once, that is, the option of removing the child from home to another placement is discounted. Indeed, as we have already suggested, some of the home on trial placements seem to have been made because there was no other more satisfactory course of action. Once this stage has been reached with difficult adolescents it is hard to see how social services departments can expect, or be expected to exercise arms-length control. As we shall see, the social workers encountered substantial difficulty in contacting nearly a fifth of the children in the Disaffected group.

Likewise, specific conditions were only imposed on just over a fifth of the placements, most of them relating to school attendance. Given that this was a group of Disaffected children as we have defined them, this seems a surprisingly modest use of conditions. Yet it may well reflect a realistic assessment of the chances of actually imposing requirements and of doing anything about it if they fail to be met. Some support for this view is lent by the fact that the proportion of placements where conditions were imposed was highest amongst the younger children and lowest amongst the older ones, as well as by the fact that in one in five of the placements that broke down the youngsters had taken independent action to move on.

It should also be recalled that 54 (36%) of the 149 children in the Disaffected group had come into care under section 15(1) of the 1969 Children and Young Persons Act whereby a supervision order is varied to a care order. It is apparent, therefore, that earlier attempts at supervising these children at home had already failed. If one adds to this the fact that the carer or carers to whom these children returned were the same as those from whom they had been removed in 80 per cent of the placements, a considerable doubt must exist about the possibility of successful supervision, especially as the children became that much older.

This argument must also apply, albeit with somewhat less force, to all the other children in the Disaffected group since, overall, three-quarters of them returned to the same carer or carers they had left when they were committed to care. One must ask what had occurred in the meantime that suggested that things would be better once they were home on trial. Fundamentally, the answer seems to be very little, except the passage of time and therefore the fact that a quarter of the children who had been committed to care for not attending school had reached school-leaving age by the time they were allowed home. However, the fact (according to the records) that during the three months before home on trial placement seven out of ten[20] of the youngsters were no longer behaving in ways that had led to the original order may have persuaded those concerned that these problems had been overcome. At least they could feel justified in supporting a placement home that was intended to lead to an application to the court for the order to be discharged.

In the event, as we have seen, these behaviours made a notable reappearance once the children were back home. Since all but 12 of the children in the Disaffected group[21] had been in residential establishments of one kind or another before going home on trial it was this form of care which appeared to have controlled or contained the behaviour that had originally given cause for concern. As one might expect, that was especially true of secure provision such as detention centres. At the same time the evidence confirms what has been found in other studies; namely, that 'improvements' achieved in residential care and in penal facilities cannot usually be sustained once children are discharged to the community and the same mechanisms of control are no longer available.[22] Only if changes have occurred in that community environment is the child's subsequent behaviour likely to be significantly altered.

A proviso to these conclusions should be added however. It may be that being in residential care does not reduce the 'troublesome' behaviour in question but rather that it keeps it from reaching official notice or leading to official action. Being home on trial may remove that 'protection'.

*   *   *

The evidence of continuity in family composition and in children's behaviour that this chapter has described must raise important questions about the justification for having committed many of these children to care in the first place. It is paradoxical, for example, that although not going to school or offending were considered originally to be grounds for removal they were not considered to be sufficient grounds for removing children a second time once they were home on trial. The evidence also indicates the apparent intractability of some of the problems associated with these children's behaviour in adolescence. It emphasises, therefore, the need to identify such problems early and for steps to be taken as soon as possible to prevent their escalation and entrenchment.

In this respect the research results offer a measure of encouragement. The relative stability of the families in the Disaffected group and the fact that few of the placements were considered to be detrimental (on our fourfold classification) suggest that much might be gained from supporting and working with the families rather than committing their children to care. We return to this theme in subsequent chapters. However, the likelihood of such a shift in policy being made is considerably increased by the changes that will accompany the introduction of the new Children Act; in particular, its insistence that courts should not impose a care order unless they are convinced that by doing so they will be making a positive contribution to a child's future wellbeing. Although the existence of the grounds for making an order will continue to be a necessary condition it will no longer be a sufficient reason.

Notes and references

1. *The Accommodation of Children (Charge and Control) Regulations*, 1988, *op. cit.* and the *Accommodation of Children with Parents etc*, 1990, *op. cit.*
2. Children Act, 1989, sections 31(2)a and b. It should be noted that the ground of 'being beyond control' will continue to be available but not the ground of being 'in moral danger'.
3. See White, Carr and Lowe, *op. cit.*, p. 81 where they say of 'beyond parental control':

   > This criterion is the one relic of the old law ... Under the old law it was possible for a parent to require a local authority to take proceedings on this ground in certain circumstances. The Government was not prepared to accept that parents should have a right to compel a local authority to take proceedings in spite of cross-bench support for such a course.

4. Only two children in the Disaffected group were under the age of criminal responsibility (that is, 10 years of age) when placed home on trial. Only one fell into this group at the end of our two-year follow-up period.
5. DHSS, *Children in Care in England and Wales, March 1984*, 1986. The percentage includes children who were on remand in care or committed for trial or sentence or detained in care.
6. Reported in 'Care Orders and Re-Offenders', in *Justice of the Peace*, 6 April, 1974. The full report was never published. Results were compared with the rates of re-offending amongst children in approved schools.

7. The objections of the magistrates were partly met in the 1980 Criminal Justice Act which allowed courts to attach a 'residential requirement' to care orders under certain circumstances. It is a provision that seems to have been little used.

8. P. Cawson, *Young Offenders in Care*, Social Research Branch, DHSS, nd.

9. M. Zander, 'What Happens to Young Offenders in Care', in *New Society*, 24 July, 1975.

10. D.J. West and D.P. Farrington, *The Delinquent Way of Life*, Heinemann, 1977.

11. M.J. Power *et al.*, 'Delinquency and the Family', in *British Journal of Social Work*, no. 4, 1974.

12. See, for a discussion of this issue, S. Jackson, *The Education of Children in Care*, Bristol Papers in Applied Social Studies, No. 1, University of Bristol, 1987.

13. DHSS, Social Services Inspectorate, *Inspection of Community Homes*, 1985.

14. N. Hazel, *A Bridge to Independence*, Blackwell, 1981.

15. It should be noted that in most cases those who attended school irregularly had been home on trial for some time: 83 per cent for more than a year.

16. M. Knapp *et al.*, *The Objectives of Child Care and Their Attainment Over a Twelve Month Period for a Cohort of New Admissions: the Suffolk Cohort Study*, Discussion Paper 373, Personal Social Services Research Unit, University of Kent, 1985.

17. 'Teenage girls' were literally defined as all those of thirteen years of age or more.

18. Amongst this group of eight breakdowns, five girls went directly to another home on trial placement; two were admitted to CHEs and one was set up in accommodation of her own. Going back further, we found that eight teenage girls were pregnant when they were placed home on trial and that in six instances that was the principal reason for the decision.

19. Central Statistical Office, *Social Trends* 14, HMSO, 1984.

20. This proportion was calculated excluding those who never left home, those for whom the question was not applicable because they had reached school leaving age, and those cases where the record was not clear (N = 128).

21. Three were in foster homes and nine had absconded.

22. For a general review of this evidence see R.A. Parker, 'Children', in I. Sinclair (ed.), *Residential Care: The Research Reviewed*, vol. II (Wagner report), HMSO, 1988.

CHAPTER 14

Disruptions

The Pattern of Placements

Although significantly fewer children in the Disaffected group than in the Protected group had been in care at some stage prior to their committal to care (38% compared with 56%) the rate was still high. However, they differed from the Protected children in respect of their routes into compulsory care. For instance, in only 14 per cent of the cases had the court appearance been preceded by a place of safety order and, as we have seen, well over a third involved the conversion of an existing supervision order into a care order.

Once in care there seemed to be a 'standard' waiting period for more of the Disaffected group before they were allowed home on trial than was the case with the Protected group. Almost two-thirds of the Disaffected group had spent between six months and three years in care or in custody. The average duration was 20 months.[1] There were fewer than in the Protected group who had been in care for brief or for very long periods. Table 25 sets out these data. However, unlike the Protected group the length of time the youngsters had been in care before their placement home did not discriminate significantly between those which were successful and those which were not.

[125]

Table 25. The Time Spent in Care or Custody Prior to Placement Home on Trial

	%
Never left home	7
Less than 6 months	14
6 months, less than a year	16
1 year, less than 2 years	32
2 years, less than 3 years	17
3 years or more	14
	100

As with the Protected group, the home on trial placements of the Disaffected group were not necessarily the first such placements the youngsters had experienced. In fact a remarkable 36 per cent of them had had a previous placement home on trial that had broken down. The great majority of these children (50 out of 54) were placed again with the same carers. Such a willingness to try again with the same carers suggests that there were compelling forces that steered the child, yet again, in that direction. One of these was certainly the difficulty of finding any satisfactory alternative, whilst another seemed to be the strong conviction that children should be at home and that repeated efforts ought to be made to ensure they were. Over and above these factors, as we shall see, there was also the determination of some youngsters to return home, even in the face of a previously unsuccessful experience.

However, such repeated attempts at placing a child home on trial have to be seen within the context of that child's care career. For example, those who were on their second or third placement back home had experienced significantly more changes of placement than those for whom the home on trial in the study was the first such arrangement. Whereas 45 per cent of the former had already had four or more placements (the record was 16) this level of disruption was reached for only 24 per cent of the latter.[2] This suggests that where children are placed home on trial 'yet again' that placement is part of a history of disrupted care careers extending over fairly long periods. Certainly, second or subsequent placements home on trial were strongly associated with unfavourable outcomes.

In general, as one might expect, the children who had been in care the longest had suffered the most disruption. For example, four out of five of those who had been in care for three years or more had had three or more placements, whereas only one in four who had been in care less than a year had been moved that often.

On the face of it the close relationship between the length of time that a child had been in care before the home on trial placement and the number of previous moves is unsurprising. However, it is important to consider whether it is the lengthy period in care that generates extra placements or whether the numerous placements lead to a child remaining in care longer. The latter would seem to be likely in the case of children who have been allowed home on trial before and where the arrangement has broken down. The breakdown of other placements may also discourage social workers from taking steps towards the discharge of the care order, particularly if those breakdowns are associated with the kind of behaviour that brought the child before the court in the first place. It may well be thought that courts would see no good reason to discharge an order under those circumstances. That, in its turn, may persuade social workers to persist with home on trial placements as an alternative, even though they consider that little purpose is actually being served by the continuation of the order. In a previous study, however, we found an example of a local authority applying successfully for the discharge of care orders (especially for adolescents) on the grounds that there was nothing further that they could offer the child.[3]

We have noted already that there was a significant difference between the Disaffected and Protected groups in respect of their accommodation prior to going home on trial. Whereas four-fifths of the former went home from residential care or from custody, that route was followed by only half of the latter. It was extremely rare (just three instances) for children in the Disaffected group to have arrived home from foster care. Of course, one of the explanations for this is that adolescents who are committed to care because of behaviour problems are less likely to be found foster homes than the younger children. Even so, when we looked at our four authorities we found that the accommodation of these older children did not correspond at all closely with the way in which all children committed to care for behaviour control reasons were accommodated. Table 26 shows this.

The biggest differences in table 26 are associated with foster care, CHEs and custody. Foster homes, as a prior placement to home on trial, are significantly under-represented whereas CHEs and custody are over-represented. The best chance of getting home on trial for the Disaffected group thus seems to have been from a CHE, a detention centre, or youth custody. The likelihood of going home on trial from a foster home would appear to be slim, although it must be borne in mind that even compared with youngsters who were committed to care for similar reasons, those who go home on trial may be the least likely to have been in a foster home. This

Table 26. The Distribution of the 'Manner of Accommodation' of all Children in the Care of the Four Study Authorities on 31.3.84 whose Status was Comparable with that of the Disaffected group in the Study and the Accommodation from which Children in the Study had Returned Home on Trial
(Excluding children who had never left home)

	Accommodation in the Four Study Authorities %	Previous Accommodation: Home on Trial Study %
Foster Care	20	2
Community Homes	26	30
Observation and Assessment Centres	15	12
CHEs	15	30
Youth Custody/ Detention Centres	8	14
Other	16	12
	100	100
	N = 1046	N = 138

may have been because of the difficulties that this group presented or because only those whom social workers considered unlikely to go home were found foster carers.

Of course, it must be recalled that some of the children in the study will have been placed home on trial in the late 70s and early 80s (albeit that they were still there in 1984) and that this was a period when CHE places were more plentiful; thus, the overall proportion of children accommodated in these homes in, say, 1980 might then have corresponded more closely with the proportion going home on trial from such establishments. The same could be argued for foster care since there has been a growth in the use of foster homes for adolescents in recent years. However, the differences in table 24 are so large that these qualifications are unlikely to invalidate the conclusions, especially when it is recalled that the average time that this Disaffected group had spent in care before the home on trial placements was 20 months. Only 15 of these youngsters had come into care before the 31st March, 1980.

As with the Protected group the question remains, therefore, why there should have been a larger flow of children going home on trial from residential care than from foster care. There is a variety of possible explanations, some of which reside in the practices of residential establishments and some that are related to the current state of foster care. However, the precise nature of these reasons may be somewhat different from those that we discussed in relation to the Protected group.

It may be that, especially in CHEs, there are longstanding traditions and expectations that at a certain point a child should be considered for return home. This was certainly the practice when, as approved schools, these establishments operated a clear-cut licensing system. Furthermore, there is evidence from Sinclair's work,[4] as we have seen, that reviews for children in residential homes are held more regularly, have more time devoted to them and involve more people (including children and their parents) than is the case for children in other forms of placement. In one in five of the Disaffected cases parents or children attended a conference prior to the child going home on trial: but all of these occurred where the child was in residential care. The fuller and more inclusive residential reviews, plus the idea that after a certain time a child deserved to go home, may be an important combination in ensuring that that happens.

We have already noted with respect to the Protected group that children in residential establishments were more likely to go home on visits or for weekends than children in foster care, and that this may well be an important influence leading to an eventual home on trial placement. However, there are likely to be other factors at work as well in particular cases. Since residential establishments shelter a disproportionate number of older and more difficult children their staff may not be sorry to see them go. Furthermore, there was evidence from the files that in residential establishments 'return home' was sometimes used as a reward for good behaviour. On the other hand there was also clear evidence in some other cases that residential staff were working purposefully and positively towards the goal of return home as part of a deliberate child-centred plan. That may suggest that residential care staff find it easier than foster parents to be fully committed to the aim of getting a child home.

It may also be that children whose care careers have been disrupted the most are both more likely to gravitate to residential care *and* towards a home on trial placement. To test such a hypothesis however it would have been necessary for us to have had information about a similar group of 'disaffected' children as those in our study who did not pass through the intermediate status of being home on trial before the order was either discharged or expired.

Outcomes

It is necessary to jump ahead somewhat in order to continue the account of the disruptions that affected the care careers of the youngsters in the Disaffected group. It will be recalled that we followed the fortunes of the children up to the end of March, 1986. By then half of the placements had broken down, adding yet another disruption to those that had occurred before. Table 27 sets out the proportions in each category of 'outcome' and also gives the comparable rates for the Protected group in brackets.

Table 27. The Outcomes of the Placements at the end of March 1986

	%	%
Placement was continuing	6	(25)
Order expired	21	(7)
Care Order, Sect.III Resolution or Wardship discharged or rescinded	23	(30)
Placement had broken down	50	(38)
	100	(100)

Several things are noteworthy about these results. First, very few (6%) of the placements were continuing as home on trial placements two years from our sampling date. That might be expected in light of the older age of the children in the Disaffected group. Indeed, in 21 per cent of the cases the order had expired upon the youngsters reaching their eighteenth birthdays. A further 23 per cent had had the order discharged or a resolution rescinded. This seems to be a low figure if home on trial is intended to lead fairly soon to the discharge of an order. It would have been reasonable to have assumed that there would have been a greater desire to discharge the care orders of the older children in the Disaffected group than those of children who had been neglected or abused, but as can be seen, this was not the case although the difference was fairly small.

Looking in more detail at the pattern of discharge of orders in the Disaffected group one sees four features. First, 35 per cent were only discharged after the child had been at home for more than two years; 35 per cent from one year up to two years and 30 per cent for under a year. Most orders were not rapidly discharged. Secondly, in every instance except one the youngsters were sixteen or over when the orders were discharged and 56 per cent were seventeen. Thirdly, in all but a couple of cases the application for discharge was made by the local authorities and in the two exceptional cases where the parents applied they did so with the backing of the local authority. No application was opposed and there were no applications by children themselves. Fourthly, there was no significant difference in the extent to which orders were discharged as between the four authorities, as between boys and girls or as between the grounds for the original committal to care.

It is tempting to regard the 50 per cent of the placements that broke down as 'failures' but in terms of our fourfold evaluation we classified only 23 per cent of them as detrimental or unsatisfactory. A fifth were regarded as 'positive'; we considered that the majority (57 per cent) had been 'adequate'. Further light on the circumstances in which placements at home ended is shed by our analysis of the principal reasons for it happening (table 28). The pattern remained much the same when we combined the primary and secondary reasons for the breakdown.

Table 28. Principal Reasons for the Breakdown of the Home on Trial Placements
(Two cases not clear)

	%
Offending	31
Breakdown in relations with carers	29
Child's request or running away	21
Not going to school	7
Other reasons	12
	100
	N = 72

(Note: no 'other' reason occurred more than twice; for example, death of the carer (2); child's difficult behaviour at home (2); neglect (2).)

It is apparent that offending, the breakdown of relationships between the child and the carer(s) and the child's decision to move away dominate the reasons for the home on trial placements terminating. However, if we look at the four main initiators of the terminations, as set out in table 29, the youngsters' decisions and actions are shown to be the most important (43%), followed by the actions of the courts (28%). What is interesting is to see the relatively minor part played by the carers and the departments.

Table 29. The Source of the Main Initiative for the Termination of the Home on Trial Placement
(Five cases not applicable or not clear)

	%
Child	43
Courts	28
Parents or Carers	17
Social Services Departments	12
	100
	N = 69

The central role played by the child in initiating the end of a placement is not so surprising when we look at their ages when the breakdowns occurred. As table 30 shows, half of the youngsters were 17 years of age when the placement ended.

Table 30. Ages of Children when the Placement Home on Trial Broke Down

	%
Under 15	13
15 under 16	13
16 under 17	24
17	50
	100
	N = 74

There was no obvious difference between these age groups in terms of the principal reasons for the termination, except that offending as a precipitating cause was most common (39%) amongst the seventeen-year-olds.

When we examined what happened next to the 74 youngsters whose home on trial placements broke down we found that 45 per cent of them (33) went directly to another placement that was classed as 'home on trial'; 23 per cent (17) went to a detention centre or into youth custody and 18 per cent (13) returned to a residential establishment in the care system. The rest went to a variety of lodgings or hostels or, as in two cases, their whereabouts were unknown.

In looking in more detail at the 33 youngsters who went on to another home on trial we found that 15 of them went to a mixture of 'friends'. This included moving in with a boyfriend or girlfriend, or with them and their parents, as well as moving in with friends of the family. The classification of some of these arrangements as 'home on trial' somewhat stretches the imagination; presumably they might just as well have been classed as 'independent living'. Furthermore, one wonders what kind of control it was possible for social workers to exercise in these circumstances. Apart from those who went to live with friends, another seven moved in with older brothers or sisters and in one case with a sister-in-law. Only six went to live with one or both parents. The remainder went to aunts, uncles, or grandparents.

However, few of these second home on trial placements in the sequence that started in March, 1984 survived until the end of our follow-up period: 26 of them broke down, often rather quickly. Of these, 19 went on to a third home on trial, but on this occasion most of them (12) returned to one or both parents rather than to friends or relatives. Ten of these third home on trials broke down and in eight cases the youngsters went to yet another home on trial placement but, in turn, seven of these broke down although only one led to a fifth home on trial placement.

The mobility of these adolescents between households, mostly within the extended family but including friends as well, was remarkable. It deserves to be studied more fully. As we have seen, the moves were mostly initiated by the youngsters themselves, albeit no doubt in response to pressures and disagreements. It seems likely that moving is regarded as a solution to a variety of problems; indeed, it would be surprising were it not, given the experience that many of these young people had had of being moved when problems became too difficult for adults to tolerate or handle. For some, 'moving on' may have become a learned response to difficulty. Even employment, when it was obtained, was typically temporary or part of a short-term training scheme.

It is, of course, tempting to conclude that 'moving on' in order to avoid or circumvent problems is a negative response that should be discouraged; but the issue is not so simple. If one has few resources (including social skills) with which to confront difficulties escape may be the only option. The task of social workers and others may be to extend those options, or at least to help make the moves as satisfactory as possible.

The discussion so far has concentrated upon those youngsters who were home on trial but whose placements broke down. It will be recalled however (table 25) that by the end of our follow-up period 44 per cent of the group were no longer in care, either because the care orders (or parental rights resolutions) had expired or been discharged. Since they ceased to be in care no records were available about what happened to them thereafter. It should not be assumed that they had settled in what had been the home on trial placement. Doubtless some moved on or were uprooted under a variety of circumstances. What little evidence we have of young people leaving care at 18 certainly suggests that this was likely.[5] That being so, the overall level of movement experienced by our Disaffected group— through early adolescence and on into adulthood—would certainly have been considerable. Going home on trial was unlikely to be a 'permanent' placement.

Of course, it is necessary to place the movements of this group within the context of adolescence in general: by 17 or 18 many young people have left home, albeit on a provisional basis. It is perhaps cause for some optimism that many of the youngsters in our Disaffected group were in contact with their extended families (many of which were both large and complicated). This, rather than the establishment of a 'permanent' place-ment, may have been an important benefit of being placed home on trial. How far solutions (or partial solutions) to some of the earlier problems that had propelled this group into care might have been dealt with within that setting, rather than by recourse to the courts, is a matter for speculation in the absence of more detailed understanding.

*   *   *

Thus, although there were some important continuities in the lives of the youngsters in the Disaffected group there were also frequent disconti-nuities or disruptions. Compared with the Protected group more of their families were intact, and more stayed intact during their absence. How-ever, although the worrisome behaviour of the Disaffected group was to some extent contained whilst in the mainstream care system or in custody it quickly reappeared once they were home, emphasising the considerable difficulty faced by social workers in exercising control in situations which are largely out of their hands from day to day.

The dominant impression left by the study of the Disaffected group was of little change apart from the high level of disruption in arrangements for their care and accommodation, disruptions that appeared to have been accentuated (and probably accelerated) by their having been committed to care. At the same time it is important to bear in mind that as these children became older they were liable to take the initiative in moving, albeit often in response to a complicated mixture of problems.

Notes and references

1. The median duration was 17 months. Both mean and median are based upon a total that excludes those who never left home.
2. It needs to be noted, however, that those children who were placed home on trial for a second or third time had been in care longer than the others so that there was more opportunity for them to have experienced more placements.
3. Farmer and Parker, *op. cit.*
4. Sinclair (1984), *op. cit.*
5. See, for example, M. Stein and K. Carey, *Leaving Care*, Blackwell, 1986.

CHAPTER 15

Why and How the Youngsters Went Home

The Reasons

Having looked at what had happened by the end of the study's two-year follow-up period it is now necessary to retrace our steps in order to consider the evidence about why the particular home on trial placements occurred. However, before we do so it is important to emphasise that that evidence was derived from the case records; that is, it was drawn from the explanations that social workers committed to paper. These explanations, or reasons were only recorded explicitly in a little over half the files. Nevertheless, the remainder furnished sufficient material for us to deduce such reasons, albeit reasons that were anchored in what was written.

A significant difference emerged in the principal reasons for home on trial as between the Disaffected and the Protected groups (table 31). It was plain that far fewer of the Disaffected group were placed home as a result of planned rehabilitation (34% compared with 50%), and that more (19% compared with 2%) arrived home because they had reached a particular juncture in their care careers; thus, for example, many young people 'graduated' home on trial when they left school or when a placement of fixed duration, such as a custodial sentence, came to an end.

There were other differences between the two groups. It was only amongst the Disaffected category that changes in the children's behaviour were given as the principal reason for returning them home. In almost all of these cases such changes were described as improvements in conduct, or as an amelioration of the problems that it had caused. By contrast, changes in the circumstances or behaviour of the parents of youngsters in the Disaffected group were much less often recorded as the main reason for the placement than they were in the Protected group. In both groups in about one in eight of the cases the principal reason sprang from pressure created by the child, although the parents' insistence that the child should be returned was much more frequent in the Protected group.

Table 31. The Primary Reason for Home on Trial Placements for the Disaffected Group
(Percentages for the Protected group are in brackets)

	%	%
Planned rehabilitation	34	(50)
Pressure from parents, child, or from within the placement, or from the court	30	(35)
Stage or age reached	19	(2)
Changes in the child's behaviour	13	(0)
Changes in the family situation	2	(12)
Other	2	(1)
	100	(100)

Of course, there were often several reasons for the home on trial placements being made. We noted what were considered to be the secondary as well as the primary factors, and when these were looked at together a somewhat different picture emerged than when the principal reason alone was examined. For example, 'planning' as either a primary or secondary reason together with another reason was noted in 38 per cent of the placements in the Disaffected group. There were 10 per cent more where it was the sole reason for home on trial. Thus *some* element of planning was evident in almost half of the cases. Where no recorded planning was detectable, by far the most common combination of reasons was for one form of external pressure to be superimposed upon another (19% of the cases); for example, pressure from the child plus pressure from the parent. It will be recalled that a similar result was obtained in the Protected group.

In the Disaffected group some form of pressure that was broadly outside the control of the social services departments was recorded as contributing to the reason for children going home on trial in nearly half the cases. However, the position of the important group where the return home was mainly prompted by the fact that the child had reached a particular age or stage falls somewhere between the notions of a 'planned' rehabilitation and 'outside' pressures. Of the 46 instances where this was either the principal or secondary reason 26 were because the child had reached school-leaving age; but somewhat surprisingly, in only 12 of these cases were the original grounds for the committal to care the child's failure to attend school. It appears, therefore, that leaving school was regarded as an appropriate point at which to return the Disaffected children home on trial, whatever the original grounds. In fact, 27 per cent of them had been placed home on this occasion between the ages of 15 years 9 months and 16 years 3 months; if the band is extended to cover the ages from 15 years 6 months to 16 years 6 months then the proportion rises to 38 per cent. Indeed, 19 children (13%) were placed home on trial exactly in the month of their sixteenth birthday. Of course, 16 was the age at which children left the care of the poor law before 1948 and, indeed, it was the upper age for a child to remain in care recommended by the Curtis committee.[1] However, it was not clear why departments were encouraged to send home children in the Disaffected group when they reached school-leaving age, or to try such a placement once more. It may simply have been a useful justification; it may have been because some residential establishments did not cater for children over school-leaving age, or it could be that it reflected a delay in returning children home in order to avoid a change of school. Yet again it might have been that reservations connected with the problems of ensuring ·school attendance were no longer relevant. Whatever the precise nature of the assumptions being made, the fact that a child in care attained school-leaving age seems to have acted as an important trigger for their being returned home on trial.

The home on trial placements were accelerated for 29 per cent of all the children in our study (if we exclude those who never left home). This is some indication of the part played by 'external' pressures, some of which may not be easy to foresee or resist. There was no significant difference between our two sub-groups in terms of the proportion of placements that were made sooner than had been intended. The main reason why 23 (62%) of the 37 accelerated placements in the Disaffected group were made was because of some action taken by the child, most frequently absconding and running home (sometimes on several occasions). By contrast, this was the case for only 6 (13%) of the 47 accelerated placements amongst the Protected group, partly no doubt because the children were younger. Parental pressure, or the threatened or actual breakdown of an existing placement, appeared to play comparatively little part in hurrying along the home on trial placements amongst the Disaffected group, whereas they did in the Protected group.

So far, we have discussed some of the recorded reasons why children went home on trial. We should mention briefly some of the factors that (according to the case records) did not seem to be important and then describe some of the formal processes surrounding the decision to allow a child home. In no case in the Disaffected group was a change in the employment situation of the parents (or other carer) or an improvement in their financial circumstances mentioned as contributing to the decision to allow a child to go home. Of other factors related to the circumstances of the families, none of the following was mentioned as influencing that decision in more than 5 per cent of the cases: the absence from the home of a specific adult; the greater involvement of the extended family; better parental health, or the carer's greater maturity and stability.

When one turns to consider the role played by the provision of extra services (other than social work) in shaping the decision to send or allow a youngster in the Disaffected group home on trial, better housing figured in 7 per cent of the case records and the availability of a special education place in 6 per cent. Apart from these two items there were no home on trial decisions in which the provision of new outside resources appeared to influence what happened.

Thus, even when the placement home on trial was 'planned' that planning did not often seem to include the mobilisation of special or extra resources for the family or a requirement that certain changes in their circumstances had to have taken place. That is not to say that changes did not occur after the placement had been made or that extra services were not made available later; we shall see, for example, that a quarter of the children in the Disaffected group attended an intermediate treatment or comparable programme at some time whilst they were at home.

The general conclusion to be drawn from these results is that just as the reasons for the Disaffected group of children being committed to care reflected concern about their behaviour, so the factors that influenced the decision for them to return home continued to reflect a preoccupation with their behaviour rather than with the circumstances of their families. This was quite different from the Protected group.

The Procedures

The absence of any record of a plan for the provision of extra services in the prelude to the home on trial placements for the Disaffected group may reflect the fact that (as in the Protected group) comparatively few people from outside the social services departments were involved in the deliberations. As we explained earlier, it was often not possible to determine from the file who attended case conferences or residential reviews prior to the placements. However, amongst the Disaffected group there was no record of a health visitor, a general practitioner, a hospital doctor or a probation officer ever being present at such meetings. One occasion was recorded when a policeman attended and one where there was a legal officer of the local authority. The virtual absence of the police and probation from the conferences or residential reviews that preceded the return home of the Disaffected group of children seems surprising given that 45 per cent of them had originally been committed to care as delinquents and that so many got into trouble with the police when they were back home.

The attendance of certain other professions in the conferences or residential reviews that occurred before the home on trial placement of the Disaffected groups was more frequent, but still not common. The presence of an educational psychologist could be identified in 10 instances and a teacher in 33. This is a relatively high figure given that so many children were either on the threshold of leaving school or had already done so. However, it is largely accounted for by the attendance of teachers employed in the residential establishments. As with the Protected group, it was rare to find a teacher present who came from the school the child would attend when they were at home. Once more these data give pause for thought when it is remembered that 36 per cent of the children had been committed to care ostensibly for not attending school.

As so many of the Disaffected group of children went home on trial from residential establishments the care staff usually attended the conferences or reviews (in 82 per cent of the cases where there was such a meeting). The residential home setting in which many of the meetings took place may also have contributed to the fact that significantly more parents attended than in the Protected group. In all, there were 29 occasions when one or more parent was present (19%). Likewise, children also attended significantly more often amongst the Disaffected group: 19 of them were involved (13%).

Although these data suggest a measure of participation by parents, children and teachers, the limited scale of both the recorded pre-placement meetings and of the information available about who attended must be re-emphasised. For only 85 of the 149 placements home on trial in the Disaffected group was there evidence on file of either a specific case conference or a residential review prior to the placement. Of these, information about who was there was only clear in 52 instances. As a proportion of all the Disaffected cases this is only 35 per cent. Hence, the findings on this matter should be treated with considerable caution. Nonetheless, if meetings did take place but were not recorded, or if there were people present whose attendance was not registered, it does suggest that social workers did not regard this information as particularly crucial or significant.

It was, however, usually clear which social services staff attended these pre-placement conferences or reviews. There were significant differences between the Protected and Disaffected groups. Whereas in 83 per cent of the meetings discussing Protected cases a team leader attended together with the social worker, this proportion fell to 37 per cent for the Disaffected cases. For these it was much more likely that the social worker attended alone. That suggests that the decisions about returning this group of children home were seen as less problematic or controversial than the Protected cases. This was broadly confirmed when we examined the level at which the authorisation for the placements was made. Whereas in the Protected group 81 per cent of the authorisations (where they could be determined) were made at the level of team leader or above, the proportion for the Disaffected group was 63 per cent. More decisions about placing children in the Disaffected category home on trial were apparently taken by field social workers (37%), suggesting that it was quite often seen as a rather routine matter that could be dealt with without the involvement of senior colleagues. Indeed, in some cases, such as going home on trial from custody, it was hardly considered to be a new placement at all but simply a resumption of the old one.

As with the Protected cases, in only a fifth of the Disaffected group was there any evidence that specific conditions were attached to the children going home on trial. The most common requirement was that they should go to school; less often that they should attend an intermediate treatment scheme. In the 31 cases where conditions were imposed they remained unenforced or only partially enforced in 13 instances. Enforcing school attendance seems to have been particularly difficult.

In only 12 cases were conditions or expectations incorporated in a written contract, although seven children had been involved in a previous home on trial placement where a contract had been drawn up. Even where there were contracts there was rarely evidence that they specified exactly what was expected during the placement or that the achievement of these targets would lead to an application for the discharge of the order. However, in five cases a decision was recorded that if the home on trial did not succeed then a long-term alternative placement would be sought for the child.

Thus, the picture that we gained from the case files was of many placements at home being made in the absence of any clearly defined, recorded and shared expectations at the outset about what, or who was 'on trial', and for what. It may have been assumed that the placement was to be a prelude to an application for the care order to be discharged; but that was by no means always entered on file or, apparently, formally conveyed to the child or the parents. As we have argued already in connection with the Protected group of children, a disinclination to make these matters too explicit or too formal may reflect the virtual absence of sanctions, short of removal, should the specified objectives or standards not be met. Likewise, the only incentives available would seem to be the provision of material and financial help or the eventual discharge of the order. Yet, in the case of adolescents it seems unlikely that any of these prospects will do much to influence their behaviour.

*   *   *

The records did not suggest that decisions about whether and when the children in the Disaffected group should go home were reached in a consistent fashion, even within the same authority. In many instances we were struck by the sense of inevitability that these children would go home on trial almost in the way that children formerly subject to approved school orders went home on licence after they had spent a certain time away. Perhaps that was why a plan for what should happen was less often to be found than in the Protected group. Certainly, the way in which the decisions were made (or at least the way in which that was recorded) suggested a rather *laissez-faire* approach in which outside influences of various kinds, rather than social work initiatives, were the key factors.

The application of the new regulations to children like those in our Disaffected group will present a major challenge if this pattern of decision-making still prevails. More people will have to be consulted and more factors systematically taken into account. Decisions will have to be taken at a senior level and agreements drawn up in all cases. On most of these counts more ground has to be made up in the case of this group than was apparent in that of our Protected group, a difference that reflects the general need for greater priority to be accorded to the development of social work and other services for adolescents and their families.

Notes and references

1. *Report of the Care of Children Committee* (Curtis), Cmd. 6922, HMSO.

CHAPTER 16

The Services Provided
and the Monitoring that Occurred
whilst the Children were
Home on Trial

Social Work

We explained in the previous chapter that few of the recorded plans for the Disaffected group included the provision of extra or special services other than social work. It is, therefore, appropriate to begin by looking at the extent of social work contacts. Merely counting the number of contacts is, as we have already acknowledged, a far from satisfactory way of describing social work inputs. However, since we were relying upon case files this was the only course open to us. The records did not contain the kind of information that would allow a more sophisticated analysis. Indeed, even the simple enumeration of social work contacts presented its problems: 30 per cent of the case records of the Disaffected group were not complete enough for the frequency of social work contacts to be calculated. Nevertheless, the distribution of average contacts over the life of the rest of the placements is of some interest and is set out in table 32, with data for the Protected group shown in brackets.

Table 32. The Distribution of the Average Frequency of Social Work Contacts
(Cases where there was no full record have been omitted)

	%	%
No contact	12	(3)
Less than monthly	33	(27)
Monthly, less than fortnightly	33	(45)
Fortnightly, less than weekly	15	(18)
Weekly or more often	7	(7)
	100	(100)
	N = 104	(N = 82)

It can be seen that in 45 per cent of the cases where full information was available there was contact with social workers on average less than monthly, and 55 per cent more frequently than that. Twenty-two per cent of the families or children were seen fortnightly or more often. Thus, there was a mixed pattern, with some children and families receiving little social work attention and a somewhat smaller proportion receiving a lot. This was broadly similar to the Protected group. However, it is clear from table 32 that a larger proportion of the Disaffected group was seen less often than monthly, or not at all. Indeed, the fact that there was no record of *any* contact for one in eight of the placements is especially disquieting, particularly given that the files in question did not seem to be incomplete. On the other hand only a slightly smaller proportion of the Disaffected group (22%) than the Protected group (25%) were contacted on a fairly frequent basis (more often than fortnightly). Of course, the average figures disguise the considerable ebb and flow of contacts that tended to characterise this group.

The various behaviour problems that reasserted themselves during the placements were often the subject of concern or investigation by or on behalf of other agencies. When children were 'in trouble' more contacts became necessary. Reports had to be prepared (for example for the courts), matters smoothed over or advice given. In this sense pressures outside the control of social workers from time to time obliged them to increase the intensity of contact as problems erupted and demands for action were made. This may help to account for the fact that there was no significant relationship between frequent visiting and a positive outcome: it tended to be the more problematic cases which generated more contact.

However, on the other side of the coin we found that social workers experienced substantial difficulty in gaining access to a quarter of the children or the families in the Disaffected group. Of the 37 placements where considerable difficulty was recorded, 27 involved elusive children. These figures do not include a number of other cases where contact was only made or maintained as a result of great persistence and ingenuity on the part of the social worker. The difficulty in seeing children or their parents was significantly related to negative outcomes and, as with the Protected cases, would seem to be an important danger signal; although what is then to be done when the signal is recognised is by no means clear.

Support Services

In most cases it was impossible to obtain a detailed picture of what the social work activity with these home on trial placements actually comprised. However, it was possible to see what support services for the child and the family the social workers had arranged. Some such help was engineered for 23 per cent of the Disaffected group, significantly less than for the Protected cases. It usually involved steering the youngster into a youth training scheme or arranging careers counselling. We recorded separately the number who took part in intermediate treatment or some similar activity and found that a quarter (26%) attended such schemes at some time whilst they were home on trial. However, there was no significant relationship between participation in these programmes and our evaluation of the placements.

As will be recalled, we only collected information on the provision of financial assistance in one authority. Here, some cash assistance was organised for the child or the family in 37 per cent of the cases (considerably less than for the Protected group where the proportion was 57%). Most payments were 'section 1' monies but, in a few cases, some small sums were obtained from charities. Financial help was mainly aimed at enabling youngsters to attend a Youth Scheme or an interview for a job. Clothes and sometimes a bicycle were also provided if they facilitated attendance at school or work.

Given the widespread poverty amongst the families and the grave difficulties which these youngsters faced in obtaining and keeping regular work once they left school it is surprising how few support services were mobilised on their behalf; particularly services or assistance that were not intermittent. However, there was evidence on the files that social workers did endeavour to obtain extra assistance from an assortment of outside agencies but that their efforts were often unsuccessful or only partially successful. It would be understandable if (as we suspect) some gave up trying or found that they simply did not have the time and energy to sustain such efforts. Cash payments, special grants and even Youth Training Schemes were typically one-off or short-term, leaving the social workers to resume their negotiations on behalf of the youngster or family once the arrangement had run its course. Long-term or persistent problems usually require more sustained assistance.

In that context it is noteworthy that special education seemed to have played an important part in supporting the placements in the Disaffected group. We included in 'special schooling' all forms of special education including centres for youngsters with attendance problems, special units within ordinary schools and separate special schools, but not CHEs. During their period home on trial 21 per cent of the Disaffected children attended such provision and a further 16 per cent had done so at some time before they went home. These were usually the older children who had completed their education by the time they returned home. Thus, overall, 37 per cent of this group of children had received some form of special education, significantly more than the Protected group and, of course, very significantly more than children in the general population. The remarkably high proportion in special education is also notable because starting special education whilst they were home on trial was significantly related to a positive outcome.

We mentioned earlier that there was only one occasion when the probation service was formally involved in the deliberations prior to the children being allowed to go home on trial. Once they were at home, however, the probation service had contact with one in eight of them. This was mainly in a supervisory capacity when they were made subject to a community service order having been found guilty of an offence. However, the probation service assumed some responsibility for about the same proportion (13%) after the care order had been discharged or expired and, in the few cases where a supervision order superseded the care order a probation officer was nominated as the supervisor.

Given the difficulties with their youngsters that many of the parents (or other carers) reported it was also surprising that (apart form social work visiting) virtually no special services or assistance were offered them. There was no evidence of steps being taken to encourage support groups, attendance at a family centre or involvement with schools or employers. Likewise, in three of our four authorities there was virtually no parent participation in the statutory reviews once their child was home.

Reviews

Excluding those who were not home on trial for a full six months, we found that regular six-monthly reviews were conducted for 41 per cent of the Disaffected group of children. (This was a higher proportion than in the Protected group where the rate was only 30 per cent). A further 27 per cent had regular reviews at some periods during their placements but not at others (48 per cent amongst the Protected cases). However, 32 per cent of the Disaffected group were not reviewed regularly at six-monthly intervals at any time during their period at home (22 per cent fell into this category amongst the Protected group). Looked at somewhat differently, 35 per cent had at least one gap in the reviews on file which was longer than 12 months, somewhat less, surprisingly, than the Protected group given, for example, that only three of the Disaffected group were on an 'at risk' register at some time whilst they were home on trial. These differences between our two groups were statistically significant but not easily explained. There are several possibilities.

One important influence may have been the fact that significant differences existed between the four authorities in terms of the regularity with which reviews were conducted. Again, taking only those cases where a child had been at home for at least six months ($N = 138$) the proportion of children in each authority who had any gap of more than a year in their reviews ranged from 56 per cent through 44 per cent and 29 per cent to 7 per cent. Likewise, in one authority none of the Disaffected group went without some regular reviewing whereas in the other three the proportions were 32 per cent, 37 per cent and 50 per cent. However, whether or not reviews were conducted regularly and as required by the legislation was not significantly associated with the outcome of the placement. Again, this may have reflected the fact that it was the more problematic cases that called for regular review and a reconsideration of what should be done.

A second explanation for the differences between our two groups may be that since (on average) the Disaffected group spent shorter periods home on trial than the Protected group (either because they left or were discharged from care) it was less likely that the passage of time would reduce the regularity of the reviewing. Certainly, for all the children in the study who were home for more than six months there was a clear and significant association between longer periods at home and the greater irregularity of the reviews. This increased notably after the first year home on trial and another jump occurred after three years.

*   *   *

The results reported in this chapter suggest that there are major questions about (a) the priority attached to work with difficult adolescents home on trial; (b) how best their parents and other carers might be supported, and (c) what special services and skills need to be mobilised or developed. The mounting sense of urgency surrounding child protection issues is liable to push such questions to the foot of child care agendas. In the very division of our sample into the Protected and the Disaffected we may contribute inadvertently to such a process. We hope not. The identification of the two groups should have made it clear that each warrants priority, albeit that different problems have to be addressed and that consequently somewhat different services and skills need to be brought to bear upon them.

CHAPTER 17

New Priorities

Antecedents

The 1969 Children and Young Persons Act abolished approved school orders. Thereafter, many of those who would have been sent to an approved school were made subject to a care order instead. In the process they became the responsibility of social services departments. The change was characterised as a movement away from detention as punishment to care as welfare, although the idea that the approved schools were part of the penal system had been played down, especially by the Home Office and by the schools themselves. In spite of that parents and children, and in many instances the courts as well, perceived committal to an approved school as a punishment. A certain period had to be spent away from home; but unless the youngsters behaved badly they were returned home before the expiry of the order. However, until it had run its full term the child or young person remained on licence and was liable to be recalled if their behaviour proved unsatisfactory.

The system was basically simple; the participants knew where they stood, even if they did not like what was happening. Whilst the children were in the approved schools the staff there were responsible for their care and supervision. The social workers in the field, the former child care officers, rarely had much contact with them. After their discharge on licence it was the job of either local probation officers or after-care officers engaged by the approved schools to carry out the supervision.

The changes that occurred in the early years of the 1970s transferred responsibility for those who would have been sent to approved schools in the past to the newly-created social services departments. Henceforth, such children could be placed in any setting that departments chose and they could be sent home on trial at any time during the life of the care order; but unless discharged earlier these orders remained in force until the youngsters were eighteen. By contrast, under the approved school system orders were made for a specific period and most would have expired before that age.

The former approved schools did not disappear as a result of these changes. They continued to be used although now called community homes with education. The youngsters who were already in the schools usually stayed on. Others went on being sent to the homes. This cushioned the full impact of the influx of adolescents upon local social services departments, although the workloads of field social workers soon began to be affected. They became responsible for adolescents who were already home on licence under the former system and for a growing number who were now placed home on trial, first to reduce the pressure on the CHEs and later in anticipation of their closure.

In effect, therefore, social workers in social services departments assumed responsibilities for many adolescents at home who had formerly been supervised by probation and after-care officers. Yet their experience was typically in work with families and younger children and, from the mid-1970s onwards, the demand increased for such work to be accorded special priority as successive child abuse inquiries forced the issue into political prominence.

Our impression is that, taken together, these changes led to the loss of the precarious foothold that had been gained in work with adolescents; a foothold which the approved school system, for all its shortcomings, had helped to establish. Some of the lost ground has been recovered, especially through the development of intermediate treatment and special fostering schemes for older children. Even now, however, there is little evidence that the experience and skills that are being developed in working with adolescents are being extended to work with them together with their families.

In terms of what the care system offers, the position of adolescents still appears to be weak. If, as tends to be assumed, the 1989 Children Act leads to fewer of the disaffected, being committed to care, matters may improve; but they could also worsen, particularly if nothing is done for those who no longer enter the care system, and if more of them end up in the penal system or as homeless on the streets.

A Future Agenda

Various suggestions, interpretations and proposals have been made in discussing the results of our study as they applied to the Disaffected group. Together, they point to some possible components of an agenda for action.

1. The evidence suggests that few lasting changes are effected by committing troublesome children to care and that, for whatever reason, doing so is likely to exacerbate the disruption of their lives. However, it may keep some of them out of trouble for a time and be preferable to what otherwise might befall them.

2. There is a measure of stability in the families which may not be fully recognised. In particular, the extended family appeared to be an important resource for some of the adolescents in our study. This may be overlooked by social services departments or remain untapped for want of appropriate policies.

3. The contribution of the extended family may be even more important in light of the clear evidence that repeated attempts to place youngsters home on trial with the same carers (usually their parents) are unlikely to succeed. That does not mean to say that a further placement elsewhere within the family is also likely to fail. Youngsters do not necessarily have to be living with parents in order to remain within the family circle.

4. It was plain that the young people in the study were both willing and able to act on their own account, albeit not always wisely. They often acted without reference to the supervising social worker, and short of bringing them back into the main care system the social workers seemed to have little power to insist that they did. Where social workers were successful in affecting the course of events they relied upon ingenuity, influence and persuasion; in short, upon gaining the trust and collaboration of the youngsters. The probability of that happening is likely to be affected by how these youngsters are treated whilst in care, especially upon the extent to which they are involved in the decisions that most profoundly affect them.

5. However, it is important to bear in mind what these young people's independent actions usually were. Typically, they involved moving. We should not be surprised that youngsters who have been moved around as a 'solution' to problems resort to that apparent remedy when they are faced with difficulties whilst they are home on trial. Frequent changes of care placements have the effect *both* of disrupting children's lives (with all that that entails) and of encouraging them to believe that disruption is the way to respond to problems, particularly those embedded in personal relationships. It goes without saying that the proliferation of care placements must be avoided: it may not be so obvious that wherever possible youngsters

need to be helped to confront and deal with problems in ways that do not automatically involve moving. Of course, that does not mean to say that moving may not be an appropriate solution in certain circumstances, but it does emphasise that that appropriateness needs to be established, and established in the light of other possible courses of action.

6. We were impressed by the significant association between special education and successful placements home on trial. It is clearly an issue that demands fuller investigation, and in the context of the overall impact of the education system on the lives of children like those in our study. Certainly, the importance of this is confirmed by the work of Quinton and Rutter.[1] Closer links between social work and education seem to promise more benefits than simply improvements in professional relationships. If that is so, the frequent absence of representatives from education (apart from teachers working in community homes) at case conferences and reviews is to be deplored. It is not only a matter of keeping schools informed of what is happening but of enlisting the resources of the education system in dealing with particular problems. For example, it was notable that in no instance did the case records refer to the involvement of counselling staff based in schools, senior teachers, educational advisers or education social workers. Perhaps the very act of committing children to care has been interpreted as a signal that the responsibility for their welfare no longer has to be shared. If that is so we must hope that the new Children Act, with its emphasis upon shared care may provide an important opportunity to dispel that assumption.

7. It is an assumption, however, that also seemed to affect the mobilisation of a range of resources. It was clear that social workers often faced an uphill task in securing the assistance of other agencies, but the records also suggested that in many instances steps were not taken to explore these possibilities. For example, some of the children in our Disaffected group were very difficult and disturbed. Yet there was little evidence to suggest that attempts had been made to provide, or to encourage them to accept, therapeutic help.

8. This may well reflect what we saw as the general problem of the relatively low priority attached to work with adolescents. Unless and until they are accorded a higher priority in social work training and research as well as policy, it seems unlikely that much progress will be made in working with the Disaffected and their families when they are home on trial. How social services departments deal with (or utilise) home on trial placements reflects trends and practices elsewhere in child care and in the welfare system as a whole. Our group of adolescents happened to be home on trial; but the issues that their care raises are not unique. What is different is their

transitional status and the continuing and explicit responsibility of the local authorities.

Notes and references

1. D. Quinton and M. Rutter, *Parenting Breakdown: The Making and Breaking of Inter-generational Links*, Avebury, 1988.

PART IV

Further Analysis and Exploration

CHAPTER 18

Further Analysis

In parts II and III we noted that a number of variables were significantly associated with our evaluations of the home on trial placements. However, this only took us so far in analysing the complicated connections between different factors. It was necessary to go somewhat further, in particular in order to identify the combined influence of certain variables and to check whether outwardly different factors were so closely related that it made no sense to treat them as if they were separate entities. The appendix explains the procedures we used to advance our analysis along these lines. Essentially, it involved the construction and interpretation of correlation matrices. What follows in this chapter is a commentary upon this further analysis. It deals separately with the Protected and Disaffected groups.

The Protected Group

In their order of correlational magnitude the eight factors that were substantially associated[1] with our evaluation of the placements as positive[2] were as follows (the correlation coefficients are given in brackets):

1. That there was no evidence of neglect or abuse during the placement (.902).

2. That no new problems emerged for the child whilst he or she was home on trial (.884).

3. That the social workers experienced no significant difficulty in gaining access to the parents or child during the placement (.658).

4. That rehabilitation had been planned during the first six months after committal to care[3] (.589).

5. That there had been no previous placement home on trial (.587).

6. That the child was under two years of age when the placement was made (.547).

7. That the parents or carers had attended reviews during the placement (.526).

8. That there had been less than a year between the order being made and the child being placed home on trial (.514).

Some of these variables showed considerable correlation between themselves, in particular 4 and 8 (.869) and, to a lesser extent, 4 and 6 (.553). As might be expected there was also a strong correlation between 6 and 8 (.741) and between 3 and 7 (.612). These correlations begin to suggest at least three 'clusters' of factors that were associated with our evaluations of the placements.[4] The first might be called the 'danger signs' cluster. It is plain that evidence of abuse or neglect, the emergence of new problems or difficulty in obtaining access to the family or child during the placement are matters for serious concern. They are alarm signals. So too is the fact that a previous attempt at a home on trial placement has been made. An early response to the first three of these signs—for example by increasing support or closer monitoring—might prevent deterioration or ensure that the child was removed in time to avoid major harm.

Some of these danger signs were, in their turn, substantially correlated with other factors. For instance, abuse or neglect whilst home on trial was correlated quite strongly (.607) with the recorded existence of concerns about the welfare of the child, other than the main grounds, when the care order (or parental rights resolution) was originally made. Similarly, the difficulty that social workers encountered in gaining access to the parents or child showed a reasonably high level of correlation (.537) with the fact that various 'external' pressures were noted as important *secondary* reasons for the placement being made (suggesting, perhaps, that when such pressure is not fully acknowledged, or where the placement is rationalised on other grounds, it should sound a note of warning).

A second group of factors seems to cluster around the broad notion of 'planning'. The results suggest that children who can be successfully rehabilitated with their families are identified early in their care careers and that steps are then taken quite quickly to achieve their return, thereby reducing the amount of disruption they suffer—at least in terms of the number of placements that they experience. These children are more likely to be infants and, perhaps surprisingly, to be kept on a child protection register for at least some time after they return home.

Of course, as we have said before, it remains unclear whether early planning for rehabilitation increases the chances of success or whether the placements most likely to succeed are those about which social workers feel confident to plan. What is apparent from our further analysis is that the existence of what might be called a disposition towards purposeful action for a particular child's return home (albeit 'on trial') is associated with its successful realisation. We need to know more about the mechanisms involved: it may be, for example, that because 'planning' was not common to all cases that it served as a means of determining priorities, either explicitly or implicitly. Certainly that seemed to be true for the inclusion of a child on a child protection register.

In this sense what is important about unevenly practised planning (or even stated intentions) is that it is likely to focus more attention and more resources upon some cases rather than others. If, as the new Children Act and its associated regulations intend, no child in care is to be without a plan for his or her future then this priority-setting function of selective planning may be lost and with it some of the apparently beneficial effects of planning for home on trial placements.

Our further analysis also suggested a third clustering of factors associated with the fortunes of the Protected group of placements. This concerned the relationship between social workers (and through them the departments) and the families. For example, the absence of any problems in obtaining access was quite strongly correlated with the attendance of parents at reviews (.612). Ease of access was more strongly correlated still with the absence of any recorded doubts about the home on trial placement being made (.756). In this there is the suggestion that the placements about which there appears to be general confidence are those where the parents or relatives do not resist supervision and where they are encouraged to participate in planning. Again, however, it is difficult to decide whether social workers and others identify early on the cases that are most likely to be successful (and *vice versa*) partly because the parents are co-operative, or at least compliant, or whether the existence of co-operative parents is an important indication that children can be safely returned or effectively supervised. As we suggested at a much earlier point, official actions that are felt by parents either to be a vote of confidence or no confidence may not only set the tone for their relationships with social workers but thereby affect the outcome of the placement.

Our attempt, through this further analysis, to trace the patterns of inter-related factors that were relevant to the success or otherwise of the home on trial placements of the Protected group should be viewed alongside the results reported in part II. Taken together they suggest that social workers can and do identify the levels of risk associated with different home on trial placements and that they operate successfully with those about which they are confident, where they have secured a working relationship with the parents and where there are few if any indications or fears that the child continues to be at great risk. The problem appears to be that a minority of placements are made where the outlook for the child is poor (and is often acknowledged to be poor); where doubts and uncertainties bedevil firm planning, and where there are negative or hostile relationships between the parents and the authorities (for whatever reasons). These are the placements that set the challenge: the challenge of whether, in future, success *can* be won against the odds with the help of more skill and more appropriate resources or whether such placements are destined to fail and should not be attempted. What is at issue is the balance between optimism and pessimism about the capacity of people to change or be helped to change. That judgement is often a fine one. It probably has to be made person by person, and certainly on the basis of as much careful assessment as it is possible to achieve.

What our further analysis of the Protected group contributes to the improvement of that assessment is the evidence that there are unlikely to be single factors that have an overwhelming significance in identifying levels and types of risk or favourable prospects. Indeed, an undue concentration upon a particular variable to the exclusion of all others in a case is likely to be misleading. The combination of indicators must be considered: some will be mutually re-enforcing whilst others may be off-setting. The importance of evidence that is confirmatory, consistent and mounting should be taken very seriously, whatever the direction in which it points. So should that which is not confirmed by other information or which is inconsistent. Indeed, these cases are likely to be especially perplexing and therefore to call for the collection of further and different information.

We were conscious throughout that the gathering and arrangement of case information are selective and partial processes and that a wealth of data, both verbal and non-verbal, may be overlooked and is likely to go unrecorded. Certainly, the study has drawn attention to a number of factors that ought to be more carefully considered; but in achieving that we are anxious not to suggest that they or any others (whether through novelty or familiarity) should be accorded a dominant place in an explanatory theory. The further analysis in particular makes it plain that one factor must be looked at alongside others, weighed accordingly and not interpreted as having a unilateral or invariable influence upon the course of events.

The Disaffected Group

As with the Protected group we list, in their order of correlational magnitude, the factors that were substantially associated with our evaluation of the Disaffected placements as positive.[5] They are:

1. That there had been no previous home on trial placement (.745).

2. That social workers experienced no significant difficulty in gaining access to the parents or child during the placement (.729).

3. That the child had spent three-fifths or more of his or her time in care (on this occasion) home on trial (.666).

4. That the child had made regular visits home prior to the placement (.547).

5. That the child had not offended whilst home on trial (.533).

6. That the child's progress whilst at home on trial had been clearly documented all or some of the time (.500).

This list displays a certain similarity to the results obtained for the Protected group. In particular, in respect to a 'danger signals' cluster of factors. Again, previous home on trial placements were a negative indicator, as was social workers' difficulty in securing access. However, for the Disaffected group 'offending' would need to be added to the cluster of warning signs. Indeed, it may be necessary to reconsider its significance as a more general reflection of other problems.

However, the items in this small cluster of 'warning' factors were substantially associated in their turn with other factors, some of which were in our list of six and some of which were not. There was, for example, a marked correlation (.769) between a previous home on trial placement having been tried and there having been no visits home prior to the placement in question. Likewise, there was quite a strong correlation (.607) between there having been a previous home on trial and concern having been expressed by outside agencies or other sources about the welfare of the child during the study placement. This may partly be accounted for by concern about school attendance problems, for these were also associated (.505) with there having been a previous home on trial placement. It was also notable that there was a marked correlation (.688) between there having been a previous home on trial and the absence of a clearly documented account on file of the child's progress during the placement in the study.

There were also moderately strong correlations both between the social workers' difficulties of access and the child's offending (.557) and their becoming pregnant (.534). Difficulty in gaining access was also sharply correlated (.788) with concern about the child's welfare expressed by outside agencies or others during the placement.

Hence, the further analysis revealed a cluster of inter-related 'warning' factors suggesting, as one might expect, that such signals are unlikely to appear in isolation but rather as a string of disquieting messages. Unfortunately, as with the Protected group, most of these messages are to be found in evidence that becomes available during the placement. That does not offer much useful guidance to those who have to decide whether or not a child should be returned home on trial in the first place, except (yet again) that a further placement home after a previous failure should be treated with considerable caution. One suspects however that the problem for social workers faced with such evidence, especially in the case of older teenagers, is to know what else can be satisfactorily provided. It may be, as we have already suggested, that more should be done to explore and mobilise the help of people other than the original carers but who remain in the child's family network.

There is also fairly strong evidence that the continuing contact of children with their families whilst they are away is associated with successful rehabilitation (.547). Unfortunately, 'visits home' (which included overnight stays) was the only information that we collected about the existence of such contact. Had we been able to gather other relevant material we suspect that a further useful cluster of 'contact' or 'preparation' variables might have been evident. Nonetheless, a few other factors were interestingly correlated with visits home before the placement. In the case of girls, this was their pregnancy whilst at home (.596), and for all the children visits home beforehand were moderately correlated (.562) with the home on trial lasting for two years or more. It was somewhat surprising therefore that given the favourable indications when there were prior visits that the care orders in these cases were not discharged sooner. However, being two years or more in the status of home on trial in the same placement was not as strongly correlated (.497) with our positive evaluations as might have been expected. On the other hand, having spent more than three-fifths of their current period in care in the home on trial placement was more highly correlated with this assessment (.666), suggesting that shorter periods away from home are linked to successful rehabilitation

Although most of the Disaffected group were teenagers when they went home there was no strong evidence to suggest that those who were under 15 were the more successful (.235) even though they had made visits home more than the older young people (.618). However, where outside agencies expressed concern about the placement this was clearly more often in connection with the younger children (.767). The younger age group had their progress whilst home on trial better documented (.504) but they were more likely to remain in the placement home on trial for more than two years (.501) and to have spent the majority of their time in care at home (.613).

These results suggest that more attention should be paid to disaggregating our Disaffected group according to their ages, even though age was not, on the face of it, closely associated with our evaluation of the placements.

It was somewhat disappointing not to have discovered additional clusterings of factors in our further analysis of the Disaffected group. Even so, what we have exposed does suggest certain important indications for practice that are connected with the maintenance of 'links' between the children and their families whilst they are apart.[6] That said however, it is important to remember that simply having been home on trial before is *not* the same thing as links having been maintained. Indeed, it appeared that these actually deteriorated between one home on trial and the next. That suggests that the quality of the relationships between parents and their children may be fairly accurately reflected by the pattern of their contacts when they are separated, always assuming, of course, that these are not impeded by official action or inaction of one kind or another.

As with the Protected group, however, we must emphasise that single factors or factors taken out of the context of their relationship to others should not be regarded as keys to better understanding even though, statistically, they may show high levels of significance or correlation.

Notes and references

1. That is, where the gamma values were more than 0.5 (see appendix).
2. Of course, the factors listed have an inverse correlation with the assessment of the placements as negative.
3. Or, in the case of parental rights resolutions, within six months of the relevant voluntary admission to care.
4. The use of the phrase 'cluster' should not be confused with the technique of cluster analysis, which we did not employ.
5. See footnote 2, above.
6. See Millham *et al.*, *op. cit.*

CHAPTER 19

Talking to Parents and Social Workers

Interviews with Parents

This chapter offers an account of the views of six families on the removal of their children into compulsory care and their subsequent return home. No claim is made that their experiences and views are representative. Nonetheless, what they have to say is illuminating. Three of the families whose voices will be heard were headed by a mother and stepfather and two by both parents. The sixth home on trial care-giver was the child's aunt.

Four of the parents expressed strong feelings about the way in which compulsory care had been taken. One mother agreed to voluntary reception into care when she was having difficulties but instead a place of safety order was taken on the children, leading to care proceedings. Not surprisingly, she saw this as

> a bit below the belt. No one really explained anything to me about a care order or anything like that. We just didn't really understand what was going on. It just came as a great shock.

In another case, after their third child was born the parents requested a short period of respite care for their two older children who had severe behavioural problems. The children's stay in care was extended on the suggestion of the social services department. However, when, after a year, the parents requested the children's return, they were shocked that instead the social services department successfully applied to have the children made wards of court.

One parent had been told by her social worker that the plan was to apply for supervision orders on her children, but in the court she found that the department was requesting care orders. She explained

> ... it was like there was two different people, one outside telling you one thing and one inside doing the opposite. I just felt like I was being stabbed in the back all the time by it. Because I couldn't believe what they were saying.

Another couple had a rather different experience. Care orders were made on their children for poor school attendance only after a series of adjournments by the court to see whether they could get the children to school and the need for care orders could be averted. However, they were not impressed by the adjournments since they considered any court action unjustified. They thought that the social worker 'had it in for them'.

For these parents, as for those in studies by Packman and Thoburn,[1] the use of compulsory care had a considerable impact, and for some it represented a betrayal of their expectations. Moreover, the committal to care seemed final and irreversible and led to profound feelings of loss. One mother's account of what the social worker told her was: 'You've lost them, there's a care order and the care order's for life'. Another said: 'As far as I was concerned I had lost my children, fullstop, and I didn't think I was going to get them back'. This mother took an overdose after the court hearing.

A mother described how she and her husband felt after the children were removed:

> When they were taken our house was like a morgue, it was like someone had died, it was so empty. Martin (her husband) was crying all the time ... he wanted to kill himself ...

Thus, whether or not the consequences of compulsory care and the parents' right to apply for the discharge of the order were fully explained, the message received by parents was initially one of hopelessness and despair.

Parents spoke with feeling of the relationship that they had with their social worker and it was clearly affected by their experience of compulsory care. One mother whose children were removed on a place of safety order had found it extremely difficult to trust her social worker. Although from the start there was a rehabilitation plan and she had regular and increasing access to her children, she could not believe that she would get them back.

(Her disbelief was compounded by her own experience of being brought up in care).

Other parents considered that the social worker who had been involved at the time of the care proceedings did not trust them enough to consider restoration. One couple felt this about their first social worker.

> But the social worker before—if we would have said to her 'We'd like her back' and all that, she would look up and say, 'Well, I wouldn't bother thinking about that yet'. She was like that.

In their view, it was only because they had later had a change of social worker that their daughter was returned to them. They felt that the new social worker was on their side. When they requested restoration, arrangements were set in motion which led to their daughter's return.[2] Mr and Mrs Ford's experience was somewhat similar. They had had to battle with the local authority to get their first child home. However, with the arrival of a new social worker whom they liked, moves were quickly made to get their second child home after a long period in substitute care. They were surprised, though, that more attention had not been given to finding out what he himself wanted.

Mr Starr had steadfastly withheld co-operation from the social services department and had not had the opportunity for a fresh start with another social worker. In order to get his children back he finally decided (with the threat of permanent alternative care for the children hanging over him) that he would have to 'play the game'. He described how he would go to see the social worker

> ... talk to her and be very polite—didn't like it mind you, being polite to her. Creep to her, like, you know.

However, his strategy paid off since when he made regular visits to the children they were allowed home for weekends. Whether this co-operation alone would have got the children home we cannot know, since in addition he had threatened legal action and this appeared to provide the final spur for the children's return.

Three of the parents got on particularly well with the foster carers of their children, and others made it clear that a good relationship with foster parents made it easier for them to visit their children whilst they were in care. In one case the children were fostered by their grandparents. The mother was pleased with the arrangement and visited regularly.

Mrs Crowther found her children's foster mother to be down-to-earth and reassuring. She told us that the foster mother would say to her: 'I can see the problems you have with Wayne—he is so much of a handful', and the foster mother added that she could 'see no reason why you can't have them home now. They shouldn't have made this care order'.

Mrs Penny, who had disliked the first foster placement, considered that the second foster parents were 'lovely' and 'backed us up quite a lot ... especially at the meetings'. It seemed then that parents found it a great help if they thought the children's care-givers were on their side and for some this may have provided a helping hand in the restoration process in terms of maintaining their morale. For parents who enjoyed a less felicitous relationship with their children's care-givers, contact with the children could be more problematic. One couple got round the difficulties they experienced in visiting their son at his foster family by seeing him regularly at the school gate.

While children were in care parents had to deal with censorious neighbours. Mrs Starr felt criticised.

> I mean I couldn't even walk up the road, people were stopping me and saying is that why your kids got took into care? And I couldn't handle it, see?

Another family had to bear unpleasant remarks from their neighbours: 'every one assumes you've ill-treated them'. However, for one couple the grapevine had a more positive outcome. The man heard that a friend's children were in care and went round to offer his sympathy. This brought them together and they subsequently married.

There was also some indication that children reacted strongly to the idea of other children staying at home if they were away. One child had apparently felt that his separation from home was a punishment, since his two younger siblings were still there. Another child who was in care had been very jealous of his mother's new pregnancy. He told his mother he hoped that she would get run over and that the baby would be killed. Fortunately, Mrs Whitcombe came to understand what lay behind her son's feelings, which was that: 'The baby's allowed to live with Mummy when it's born, he wasn't allowed to live with Mummy'.

On the whole, parents displayed a fairly good understanding of the situation of home on trial.[3] Mrs Whitcombe put it this way:

> He was home on trial to see how I went along. If things went well it would go back to court to have the care order taken off and then a supervision order placed on again ... I know that he can be removed at any time.

One mother gave a rather apposite example of how her social worker discharged the local authority's parental responsibilities for her child. She described how, after she had had a drinking lapse, the social worker had checked that the children had nonetheless been properly fed and the house cleaned. For Mrs Crowther, it was clear that home on trial meant that 'the care order would be on. They've got the legal right to the children'. To her the trial made her feel like a 'criminal'. Mr and Mrs Penny remembered the home on trial agreement form they had signed. To this mother it meant being 'prepared for people to keep coming up and calling on you'. They had asked their social worker if the home on trial meant a temporary or permanent placement with them and understood it meant that the children 'were coming home permanently but on trial, sort of thing, so that if it doesn't work out they [the social services department] can take them back again'. For Mrs Penny, in practice, it had meant accounting for every mark and bruise on the children.

Mr and Mrs Ford considered that the aim was for their daughter to stay with them permanently and that, in due course, the wardship would be discharged. However, they were not fearful that their daughter would be removed since they knew that her behaviour had made her impossible to contain in a care placement. Their understanding of wardship was expressed thus: 'You don't feel they are properly yours—but social services is not really in control'.[4] For the relative who had her sister's child with her, the idea of a trial had the positive effect of reassuring her that 'if he gets too much out of hand then she'll [the social worker] have to take him back'. It was apparent, then, that the term 'home on trial' was recalled by parents and served as a reminder to them that the local authority retained powers to supervise and to remove children if necessary.

The existence of the care order was sometimes also seen as beneficial. For David's aunt it offered the assurance that her nephew could not return to his mother without the permission of the social services department. For two mothers the care order had also been useful because it had served to protect them from the demands of the birth fathers for custody and access. The social workers had reinforced the mother's custody and reduced or stopped the father's access. Clearly social workers can offer help through their powers under the care order in relation to the absent partner, and when such help was offered it was greatly appreciated.

The children had been away from their parents in substitute care for periods from eight months to five years. The exception was the child who, when removed from his parents, was placed immediately with his aunt. Since there were no foster payments, this was classed as a home on trial placement.

Although all the parents wanted their children to be returned, and all had maintained contact with them, two sets of parents felt that the actual placement was a case of the children being 'dumped' back with them. This expression appeared to be used to convey a lack of preparation for the reality of the experience of the children's returns and the absence of advice or help in managing them. One mother said: 'It wasn't explained that it would be difficult to cope with, or any of this ...' It appeared that regular stays with their parents before going home on trial did not lessen the impact of the children's return.

Thus, when difficulties arose they sometimes had the added element of being unexpected; and difficulties did arise for all the families. One mother graphically described how, after nine months' separation, she had forgotten how to change her baby's nappy.

> I just sat there and Sharon needed changing, and I thought, what do I do? I just couldn't think how to go about changing her. I said to Steve [her husband], 'Steve come and change her, show me what to do again'. I mean it's like having a baby for the first time—you're sort of so wary and so gentle about how to pick them up and it was just like that all over again, and it frightened me ... I just sort of panicked.

The separation had a profound effect on her and a year after the children had returned she could still say:

> It feels that we're just looking after the children for somebody else. It don't feel they are mine again. But everything seems to be slowly improving, so we've just got to wait and see what happens.[5]

She had had the feeling that the social services department would come in and remove the children again:

> I think about a month or two went by and I was expecting them to say 'Right, time's up, they've got to go back'. And I think it's only now really, after a year, that it's sunk in that I have got them home permanently.

Her children's behaviour may, to some extent, have reflected her fears, since they were still 'very, very clingy'. It was hard for her to go out without the children because they found such separations difficult. Her three-year-old son still had tantrums if there was a stranger in the room and his mother went out for a moment. When she returned 'he will just sit on my lap and he will cling to me and he won't let me go'.

Mrs Whitcombe described the return of her eight-year-old son after two years living with foster carers: 'It was like me and Shaun had to learn to live with each other all over again'. Shaun had very much wanted to live with his mother but problems of control soon arose. At first he would only eat beefburgers which he had become used to at the foster parent's. His mother considered that he was testing her: 'It was sort of, how far can I push Mummy before she tells me off? Yes, I think he was testing me'. This mother had given in to her son a great deal before the care proceedings and now she had to establish a different pattern of discipline. These difficulties came to a head one day when Shaun was sent to his room for misbehaving and would not stay there. After Mrs Whitcombe locked him in, Shaun threatened to jump out of the window. His mother went in and took his clothes out of the wardrobe and said that if he was not happy he would have to return to his foster home. Shaun struggled to take the clothes back from his mother and begged to stay. When this situation was resolved the mother felt that an important landmark had been reached in terms of establishing that she was in charge.

Mr and Mrs Penny had to face a lot of behaviour difficulties when their daughter came home after a year in care. She went through a phase of biting people; she fought with other children; threw tantrums and wet the bed. She showed a lot of jealousy towards her siblings (one of whom was a new baby) and defiance to her mother. Despite help from the social worker and a child psychologist, the couple felt unable to cope with this behaviour. A year after she returned to live with them they requested that she be permanently removed.

One couple knew that their daughter was proving extremely hard to handle whilst away from them. She had been received into care because of her behaviour problems and returned, five years later, older and harder to handle. She was boisterous, overactive and destructive. She fought with her sister and did not go to sleep until late. She also had severe temper tantrums, sometimes in public. Similarly, another parent had to cope with her son's recurring nightmares and bed-wetting. The bed-wetting was a major problem and only started to improve after 18 months, whilst the nightmares still occurred intermittently.

Parents reported that they did not receive much practical help from social workers in managing their children's behaviour. In some cases this was because they feared that asking for help would be seen as a sign that they were not coping and the consequence might be the children's removal. One mother who did ask for help by telephoning the social services office was disappointed that no alternative was offered when her social worker was unavailable. She wanted a special service to be available to help settle children back. Her preference was for help to be available from an impartial source, preferably from a group of parents who had themselves undergone these difficulties. She and another mother interviewed both said they wanted a group of this sort. As she put it, she wanted

someone to talk to. You need someone to turn round to and say, 'Well look, I can't handle this, how do I go about it? It's getting too much for me. I don't want them to go back into care again'.

Parents also welcomed the occasional break from caring for the children. Children's attendance at day nursery was obviously a help and in one case led to an improvement in the child's behaviour. Two mothers had friends who could look after their children at times if the favour was returned. In three cases it appeared that the husband had actually given up work primarily to give his wife support with the children. David's aunt turned to her mother for an occasional much-needed overnight break from her charge.

In two cases it was reported that social workers had set conditions for the children's return. In one, where the issue was school attendance, the conditions concerned the children's cleanliness and bedtime, as well as attendance at school. For another parent, who had physically abused one of her children, conditions were laid down about the family accepting frequent visits from the social worker and health visitor. In the event, the health visitor visited regularly for three weeks and then her visits tapered off. The social worker established a pattern of weekly visits in which she drove one of the children to a group activity. The parents were relieved by the infrequency of visits but somewhat perplexed. As they said, 'We're happy, but at the same time you do expect her, being a social worker, to come in. They created a fuss in the first place then they show no interest afterwards'. Mr and Mrs Crowther had recently been introduced to their new social worker. He had not visited since. Mrs Crowther was trying to make sense of it: '... so I don't know whether they're giving us a lot of play, or what'. It seems that the pattern and nature of social workers' contacts with parents, including the absence of visits, are interpreted in their own ways by families. A more explicit schedule of visiting, if adhered to, might be appreciated.

Sometimes financial problems were mentioned. One family was worried about their financial situation because the father was considered to be out of work voluntarily and part of his benefit had been stopped. They had not asked their social worker for help because they felt so grateful for the daughter's return and for the help that they had already received. Mr and Mrs Ford had received some material help but would have liked more financial aid. They saw their lack of money as a major problem, not least in not being able to occupy their difficult and very active child. David's aunt had debts and court orders for arrears of payments. She was receiving no financial help from the social services department who had requested that she look after her nephew. When she had asked her social worker for a foster care payment she had told her that this was not possible. 'I'm sorry', she said, 'we cannot change the law'. In fact, the local authority could have paid her a fostering allowance.

Two of the families were fairly classic cases of 'planned rehabilitation'. In one, the children had originally been removed because of physical abuse and in the other because of neglect due to the mother's drink problem. In one family the parents were immensely grateful to the social worker for returning the child and in the other very relieved to find that they did get the children back. Both sets of parents were very anxious for the home on trial to work and fearful that the children would be removed again. The control which the social worker exercised was underpinned by the power to do this and by the families' desire that it should not happen.

In two other families the picture was, however, less straightforward. One was a family where the children were removed for physical abuse. The parents, far from being fearful that the children would be removed from their care during home on trial, turned the tables by requesting that the social services remove one of the children and arrange permanent alternative care for her. This was because of her behaviour and in particular because of its effect on their other children. It occurred in spite of the help which they had received to deal with the problem. Another mother battled to have her children returned home on trial. However, only six months later she left her husband and the children. In these two situations social workers were supervising placements in which parental motivation to care for the children was less consistent.

Finally, in the other two families the social services department was in a sense beholden to them for looking after the children. One was the aunt who was looking after her nephew to prevent him from having to go into a substitute care placement. The other was a couple whose daughter's behaviour had become very difficult to manage and, according to them, the foster parents eventually 'could do nothing with her'. The parents found her difficult but the home on trial placement held. They had no fears that she would be taken away since as they put it, 'they could never take her back, they can't do a thing with her anyway'.

Comment

The interviews with parents thus illustrated the quite different bases on which home on trial placements can operate. In some cases parents were only too anxious to prove that they could be good parents to their children and become fully responsible for them. In others, the motivation or ability to resume full parenting responsibilities was less consistent, and as a consequence parents might request or allow their children to return to the care of the local authority. In yet other cases parents or relatives undertook to have the children with them in the full knowledge that the local authority would either be reluctant or unable to place them back in care. Thus the balance of power in these placements was sometimes firmly with the social worker and sometimes not.

Overall, these interviews offer some illumination of the experience of parents whose children are returned home on trial. They show once again the effect that compulsory care can have on parents and their deep sense of loss when their children are removed. The language parents used in interview ('a stab in the back', 'a bit below the belt', 'it was like someone had died') suggests that the events could be experienced as a traumatic assault, and their accounts show that they saw the whole process of removal as having considerable influence on the processes of return. Unfortunately, we do not have accounts from children to show the impact of the experience of separation on them.

The interviews highlight the importance of preparation for the children's return; the serious problems of readjustment faced by children and their families; and the crucial need for advice and help to cope with these difficulties, not least with difficult child behaviour. They also illustrate the varying amounts of leverage which social workers may have in supervising home on trial situations. This suggests that broad generalisations about home on trial may be misleading and that it is necessary to pay attention to the differences which exist among home on trial placements and the implications of these differences.

The Social Workers' Views

Interviews were conducted with the social workers who were responsible for the six families who had been seen. In only two instances had they been involved in both the application for compulsory care and the making of the home on trial placement. In both these cases the children's removal had provoked a great deal of hostility. This had included verbal aggression and in one case the social worker had been assaulted. The hostility had been worked through with one family. As the social worker said:

We got there in the end in some ways ... simply because I stayed with it ... And in a sense she could and did throw whatever she wanted to at me. But ... all right I will still go through that.

For the other families there had been a change of social worker whilst the child was in substitute care or at the start of the home on trial placement. Thus, whilst the parents had a complete knowledge of events from the start, the social workers often had not. The familiarity of social workers with the children's case histories was variable, but for some a focus on the present seemed to have excluded a full reading of the past. In one instance the worker was unsure of the conditions that had been laid down for the home on trial placement.

Social workers put far less emphasis than parents on the effects of compulsory care on the families—and, of course, in many cases the current social worker had not been involved at that stage. An exception was provided by one social worker who was very clear about the difficulties that were created. She had recommended voluntary care but compulsory care had been used because of the mother's adverse reaction to a police interview which the worker had attempted to prevent.

The reasons for the child's return home on trial were not always seen in the same way by social workers and parents. One social worker considered that it was precipitated when permanent care was threatened. This was also the mother's view. The social worker added that the ending of the children's first foster placement because of the foster mother's illness was another factor. However, no mention was made of the solicitor's letter querying the parents' lack of access, which the children's mother believed had helped to shift things in her favour. For another family in which the mother believed that her daughter's return had been the result of a positive attitude on the part of her new social worker, the worker herself considered that the initiative had arisen from the mother and the foster mother, and that she had merely lent her endorsement. Another family who attributed their daughter's return to the efforts of their new social worker to get her home, did not mention the girl's own insistence that she wanted to return and that she had shown by her behaviour that she would brook no alternative. However, both the parents and the social worker agreed that another contributory factor in achieving the placement home on trial was the child's adverse experiences whilst in care.

One factor which we can see that parents viewed as crucial to their child's return was the social worker's confidence in the family. The interviews with the social workers also showed how important this could be. In one case a mother had shown bizarre and punitive behaviour towards her children. The social worker's assessment was that home on trial could work even though the mother had refused to accept psychiatric treatment. Clearly an insistence on psychiatric treatment could have led to a position of stalemate. In spite of the difficulties of working with the mother, the social worker was willing to back her own judgement and work towards home on trial. She could see, however, how another view could have been taken: 'if you had taken a particular line it would not have been difficult to see these children remaining in care'. Another social worker also emphasised the importance of setting realistic goals:

> I think you have to always accept there are some things you are never going to change, and once you've accepted that, then perhaps you can work in a positive way with the things that you maybe can change.

The examples suggest, as does the case material, that particularly when there are doubts about the wisdom of a home on trial placement, a child's chances of being so placed may depend on social workers' commitment to achieving it, together with their willingness to invest the necessary time.

Social workers had taken trouble to explain to the carers the legal position of the home on trial placement. Only one had felt it necessary to play down the implications of the local authority's legal powers. This worker considered that the power of removal 'makes it sound . . . more frightening than it is in practice'. In fact in this case a greater willingness to use authority might have led to an earlier home on trial being made. In general, however, the social workers had not shrunk from emphasising the extent of their powers under the care order and they used the term 'home on trial' to assist in the explanation. One social worker described how shocked a mother was to find out that when her children returned the care order continued; she had expected that it would end at that point.

In most cases the difficulties which families had encountered after the child's return were underestimated by the social workers. This is not entirely surprising since some families had been at pains to keep these facts from them. Social workers tended to say that children had settled back very well and fairly easily, and this included even the workers with whom the parents had discussed the difficulties which arose. This was in contrast to the parents' own accounts. Social workers tended not to mention the children's behaviour difficulties nor the serious concerns that parents had described in great detail during the interviews with us. This suggests that social workers may not be aware of the extent to which parents put on a brave face in order to show them that they are coping.

Social workers mentioned the importance of continuity for children and, when possible, arrangements had been made for children to attend the same day nursery or school while in care as they had done when at home. This had been possible in four cases. Some social workers had spent a great deal of time and effort to bring about the home on trial placement—'an extremely time-consuming piece of work' as one put it—sometimes with additional help from other sources such as a family support centre. During the placement, visits to a family (at least in the beginning) could be twice weekly or more often. In two cases the social worker had regularly provided transport several times a week, in one case in order to ensure the child's attendance at day nursery and in the other to ensure that a child went for psychotherapy. Day nursery attendance was made a condition of home on trial in the two families where there were children under five, and other services such as assistance from a home aide, a child psychologist, a psychotherapist or a day special school were employed when needed.

The social worker's descriptions of these high levels of input formed something of a contrast with the parents' accounts of needing more help. Thus one mother who had been visited twice a week, reducing to every ten days, had complained that she could not get help when she telephoned if her social worker was out of the office. Clearly access to help on demand was important to her. Another couple who were given quite high levels of outside services nonetheless appeared to want more specific help in child management. It may be that in some cases parents had not felt able to voice their needs or that the services which they were offered were not appropriate or sufficiently responsive to their requirements.

For some of the social workers, working towards the discharge of the order appeared to be important. One social worker said that her aim during home on trial was to get to a position where the care order could be removed and replaced with a supervision order, and the children's names taken off the child protection register. She saw this as working towards returning power to the parents. In another case a written contract for the home on trial placement was on file which included an agreement that the social services department would consider discharging the care order within a short time if the placement were successful. (However, this contract had been drawn up by a predecessor, and the social worker only discovered it when preparing to see us). In a third case the mother was very aware that the care order would be discharged and replaced with a supervision order when and if she succeeded in giving up alcohol for a considerable period, and in a fourth the social worker's stated aim to us was to see the child removed from compulsory care. Such a focus on working towards the discharge of the order was less evident in the case-file study. Whether this was because such practice was infrequently recorded in case notes we do not know.

During the home on trial placements some social workers had used the authority of the care order to good effect. One had got a mother to remove a bolt from her child's bedroom door and another had used the threat of removal to get the mother to stop drinking when she had a relapse. However, in another instance the social services department's attempt to effect change by threatening to take compulsory action had failed. The department had progressively and over time obtained supervision orders on all the children, threatened to obtain care orders, and finally resorted to care proceedings, all without managing to get the parents to take the children to school. It was only, so the social worker explained, when the subsequent threat of long-term care seemed real that the parents began to work towards their children's return. It was also interesting to note that while social workers sometimes mentioned that children were on the child protection register, parents never did.

The significance to children in care of having siblings who return home was underlined by the social worker's account of one family. Susan and her sister had been removed and placed in care. After three years her sister was spending increasingly long periods at home whilst Susan's own access visits were reduced. Finally, her sister returned home permanently and Susan's visits were stopped entirely. Susan was fostered with a view to adoption, but in the social worker's words, 'the girl knew that that's what the plan for her was, but she didn't accept it. She never, ever accepted why she couldn't go home, particularly with her sister there'. The girl reacted by raising the stakes. She displayed violent behaviour, temper tantrums and aggression, alternating with withdrawal and crying. She 'didn't want anything to do with the foster parents [and] upped her demands about "why can't I go home?" ' This led to a reconsideration of her situation, as a result of which she was placed at home where she remained. Her behaviour calmed down once she got home, 'she went from a scale of about 120 down to about 40. It was quite remarkable'. The social worker had concluded that in such circumstances, unless the home situation was very poor, home on trial had to be tried.

Comment

Thus, the interviews with social workers made an interesting comparison with those of the parents. Generally, the families put far more emphasis on the effects of compulsory care than did social workers, and the extent to which this was still a live issue to parents may not have been appreciated by them. There were also some differences, as well as some overlap, in the perceptions of parents and field workers as to what had brought about the home on trial placement. In two cases where the families had seen the social worker as instrumental, the workers themselves attributed the main initiative to the child or the family. An important finding was that social workers greatly underestimated the extent of the difficulties that parents had encountered in coping with their children on their return. Whilst parents had described severe and enduring behaviour difficulties, social workers tended to say that children had settled back fairly easily. It appeared that social workers may not always be aware of the extent to which parents conceal problems in order to try to show that they are able to cope.

Parents tended to say that they needed more advice and support than they had been given in dealing with their children during home on trial placements. Yet they had often received a considerable number of visits as well as other services. It may be that the services offered were not tailored to the family's view of their needs and possibly that specific practical help and advice with behaviour difficulties was lacking or could not be acted upon. The social work interviews made apparent the considerable time and commitment that was needed to achieve the home on trial placements and then to maintain them. Some of the social workers saw working towards the discharge of the order as an important aim. Most of them reported using the authority of the care order quite explicitly, albeit by the threat of removal rather than by actually carrying it out This had also been reflected in what the parents said.

Notes and references

1. Packman, *op. cit.* This study emphasised the conflicts which arise between parents and social workers when children are removed from home under compulsion. It also points out that some parents feel betrayed by social workers when they shift without warning from a helping to a controlling role. The study concludes that when possible voluntary care should be the preferred route to care. See also Thoburn, *op. cit.* But note, in contrast, that Fisher *et al.* (*op. cit.*), found that for the parents of older children compulsory care could represent a relief rather than a trauma.

2. Thoburn, *op. cit.* In this study too, it was shown that the arrival of a new social worker could lead to rehabilitation.

3. This is similar to Thoburn's findings (Thoburn, *op. cit.*).

4. This may have been a reference to the fact that all decisions had to be taken to the wardship court for approval.
5. This reaction was also noted by Thoburn in her study, *op. cit.*

CHAPTER 20

Themes and Issues

In reviewing the results of the research a number of issues and themes stand out. We discuss them briefly below, although each raises far-reaching matters that must continue to concern those who are involved in child care policy or practice.

Disaggregation

Concepts and categories are convenient for organising complicated phenomena. A child who is classified as 'home on trial' looks, on the face of it, to occupy a simple and straightforward status. What became apparent early in our study was that this designation covered numerous circumstances and conditions, some of which were so different from each other that it was misleading and unhelpful to gather them together in a single administrative category.[1] We worked throughout with a division between those children whom we called the 'Protected' and those whom we termed the 'Disaffected'. However, that was only a first step in the disaggregation that is needed in order to create categories that more closely resemble reality. We believe that there are important distinctions between, say, the fortunes of neglected and abused children when they go home on trial as well as differences in the way that social workers may have to approach the issues of their support and supervision. We also believe that it would be helpful to treat separately children who go home to parents from those who are placed with relatives and, especially, those who go to 'friends' since many of these friends are boyfriends or girlfriends of much the same age as the child in care. In short, we must not assume that home on trial placements form an homogeneous group: they do not.

New Regulations

We have already made reference to the Charge and Control regulations that came into force in June, 1989[2]. They specify what social services departments must do in relation to the placement and supervision of children who, in the past, have been referred to as being 'home on trial' and sometimes as being 'home in care'. No such regulations existed before and thus their implementation is likely to have an important effect upon the pattern and supervision of such placements. From the evidence of our study the most significant features of the new regulations are the requirements that consultation and notification should take place with various individuals and bodies before a placement is made; the requirement that the child must be visited at least as frequently as the specified intervals,[3] and that in carrying out the statutory reviews a local authority should (amongst other things) address the questions of whether the placement continues to be the most suitable for the child in the circumstances and whether an application should be made for the care order to be discharged. A register of 'charge and control' children now has to be kept by all local authorities. We consider that these requirements are particularly important because, singly and together, they will ensure that more regular attention is paid to the condition of being home on trial. Incidentally, the regulations make no mention of a 'trial' although the idea seems to be implicit in injunctions such as that the authority should remove a child if his or her wellbeing or safety is in jeopardy.

As a result of these changes 'charge and control' placements have been put on a similar footing to other kinds of placements as far as their regulation is concerned. Certainly, this should enable local authorities (and the Department of Health) to monitor what is going on better and, from a researcher's point of view, it will ease considerably the problems faced by any subsequent study of the subject.

However, to return to our previous point about the need for the critical appraisal of established categories it must be noted that the regulations are framed as if they were equally appropriate for all charge and control arrangements. Plainly they are not. They are better designed for application to our Protected group than they are to the Disaffected; for instance, how will a local authority obtain references for the 'carers' when adolescents simply take matters into their own hands and move to another household? Nonetheless, despite such difficulties the very existence of regulations will, we believe, do much to promote procedures that bring 'home on trial' out of the policy and practice backwater in which we found it when we first contemplated this research.

The Charge and Control regulations will, however, be short-lived. The implementation of the 1989 Children Act[4] requires them to be modified and that has created the opportunity to make other changes in the light of experience. An outline of the revised and re-named regulations has appeared as a consultative document entitled *Accommodation of Children with Parents.*[5] The principal differences between what is proposed and the existing regulations are fourfold. First, the concept of 'charge and control' disappears. This 'reflects the new position after a care order is granted whereby the parents do not lose parental responsibility although a local authority acquires it and the power to limit the parents' exercise of their responsibility'.[6] The change is in line with the new principles upon which the Act is based. Secondly, the placements of children who are on care orders with their relatives or friends will no longer be subject to these regulations but instead be governed by those that deal with foster placements (unless, that is, a residence order has already been made). Thirdly, short-term stays of 24 hours or more are intended to be covered by the regulations. Finally, the placements of children who are on remand but accommodated by a local authority will not be regulated by the new statutory instrument.

These proposals are likely to modify yet further the classification and approach to what were originally referred to as 'home on trial' placements. For example, the requirement that the placement of children in care with relatives should be subject to the fostering regulations will make it difficult for local authorities not to treat such relatives (or friends) as foster parents who are eligible for the appropriate allowances. Certainly the inclusion of short-term placements within the scope of the regulations will increase the number of children who are classified as 'accommodated with parents'. Had we included such short-term cases in our study the results might have been somewhat different. Indeed if, in future, we are to appreciate the whole picture of placements with parents it will be essential to be able to identify their duration and their frequency.

Last but not least, the fact that under the new Act parents will continue to have responsibilities towards a child who is subject to a care order (albeit these may be curtailed in certain circumstances) is likely to make it clearer who is to be held accountable for what when such a child is 'accommodated with parents'. Indeed, the consultative document explains that it will be up to the local authority 'to define clearly in the placement agreement to what extent the carer has delegated responsibility to take decisions'.[7] That will lead to different conditions and responsibilities being set for different families. Even so, it will not eliminate the problem of sanctions. For example, schedule 2 to the proposed new regulations lists 'the particulars on which there should be agreement with the person with whom the child is to be placed'[8] and included amongst them is the requirement that the local authority should be notified of changes of address, changes in the household or any serious occurrences involving the child. What if these or other stipulations are not observed? A failure to do so will not necessarily indicate that the child should be removed in his or her 'best interests'; but no other sanction really exists. Likewise, the schedule makes clear that the agreement must include a specification of what the local authority will be responsible for (for example, the child's health and education needs). What if it fails to fulfil these undertakings? Will the parents be able (or willing) to obtain redress through the complaints system that all authorities are now obliged to establish; through the Ombudsman, or through the courts?

Authority, Control and Skill

The status of home on trial exposes more vividly than most other arrangements for the child in care the severe limitations that exist on the exercise of effective control through authority. The day-to-day care of the children is in the hands of parents (and sometimes others) who are neither the agents nor the employees of the local authority and whose capacity to provide adequate care or control has previously been put in question. As we have already pointed out several times, the only specific sanction that social workers possess is the removal of the child; but this is something that they are reluctant to do, and even the threat of its use may undermine the rehabilitative work that they are trying to accomplish. Even so, parents are conscious of the sanction and some are certainly fearful that it will be invoked. It can feel oppressive even though a local authority has little or no intention of resorting to removal.

Thus most of the time social workers have to contrive a complicated mixture of ways of working in order to control, support and monitor difficult and potentially harmful family situations. As we noted earlier it is essential to recognise the reality of the structure of power in home on trial placements, both within the families as well as between social workers and parents or children. The social workers' authority does not necessarily confer upon them a comparable power.

The study impressed upon us the great skill that social workers need in working with home on trial arrangements; even more, we would suggest, than when they work with foster placements. Yet fostering work (together with adoption) is frequently seen as requiring particular skills that have to be developed by training and practised by special teams. Despite the emergence of all kinds of new specialisms in social work, as far as we know no specialism in restoring children to their families has been suggested. That will surely have to be re-considered; after all, there are some 10,000 children home on trial at any one time and many more than that in a full year.

Judgement and Action

As we have seen there is a good deal of evidence that from the start social workers accurately identify those home on trial placements which are likely to prove most detrimental to the child. Nonetheless, these placements were made (or allowed). This suggests several things. First, it may be that even those placements which social workers consider least likely to be successful still, in their judgement, have a sufficient chance of success to warrant going ahead. Secondly, it may be that the marginal placements are made because no other option appears to offer a better chance of success. Thirdly, as we have suggested on several occasions, it may be that the re-unification of children with their families is regarded by social workers (and indeed by others) as such a strong imperative that a higher level of risk is accepted in order to win the greater prize for some children; almost on the principle of nothing ventured nothing gained. After all, a substantial proportion of all home on trial placements are successful. Fourthly, placements that carry identified high risk may nonetheless occur because matters are largely out of the control of social services departments. These placements (and the study provides examples) are neither 'made' nor 'allowed': they are accepted or tolerated as *faits accomplis*.

It is likely that all four of these explanations of why some dubious placements occurred have validity and, indeed, that in a number of instances they operated in combination. Nonetheless, we need to know much more about their precise nature and how they influence home on trial decisions— even the decision to accept a *fait accompli*. In short, in order to be helpful we need to understand better the processes whereby judgements are formed and which judgements are translated into action and why.

However it would be misleading to concentrate only upon the way in which judgements are made in the most marginal cases. It must be borne in mind that we considered that 44 per cent of the full sample of 321 home on trial placements offered the child a positive experience and that a further 35 per cent were assessed as at least adequate. We do not have comparable figures for similar children in other forms of care. Nonetheless, research has usually found rates of 'failure' in foster homes lying somewhere between 20 and 50 per cent.[9] Given the acknowledged risks in some home on trial placements the 'success' rate in our study compares quite favourably with these foster care proportions. However, it will be recalled that for the Protected group our original four-fold evaluations assumed a U-shaped distribution. That is, on the one hand there was a quite sizeable group for whom the placement home on trial was positive whilst on the other there was a smaller but significant group for whom it was detrimental. Relatively few of the placements of Protected children fell into our two intermediate categories. This was not the pattern in the Disaffected group. This suggests that at least for children like those in our Protected group further detailed research may make it possible to identify more precisely those situations in which they are likely to suffer detrimental experiences if they go home. Conversely, it ought to be possible to identify the group for which the prospects are most favourable. Of course, there will always be a group in between where the indications are ambiguous or at least mixed.

Ambiguity and Paradox

We were struck by the ambiguities and contradictions surrounding home on trial. The local authority held parental powers whilst the parent had day-to-day care of the child. This left an area of uncertainty about who, for example, had responsibility for getting the child to school or, if the child injured someone, who would be responsible if a claim for compensation were made. Under the regulations some of these issues can now be clarified in the placement agreement, but others are likely to remain.

The situation of home on trial, unlike any other child care disposition, entails the crucial paradox that whilst the local authority holds maximum responsibility for the child it has very little control over what actually happens. It might be thought that this would lead to a sharp focus on these placements. Yet the opposite appeared to be the case. The resources made available to substitute families, including financial support, were withheld from this disadvantaged group of families. Furthermore, the status of home on trial, which is commonly regarded as a prelude to permanence, frequently continued for long periods and thus itself created a protracted state of impermanence.

These contradictions appear to reflect contradictory aspects of the home on trial status itself. Not only that, but they appear to reflect the inherent tension between the desire on the one hand to rescue children from harm and the wish on the other to respect the integrity of the family which ultimately lies at the heart of restoration. Social workers who consider restoring children have to manage these tensions without having clear guidance as to how best it should be done. Indeed, in weighing up these children's life chances the decisions that they reached could often be open to criticism from one side or the other of these contending considerations.

Care Careers

The study has highlighted the importance of viewing any particular episode or placement experienced by children in care as part of a career or history. Before this research we, and indeed many others, tended to regard a home on trial placement as a discrete episode and one that usually foreshadowed the end of a child's period in care. In the event the study revealed a sizeable minority for whom there had been a similar episode before and for many others the home on trial placement continued for a considerable time or was followed by another such placement.

It is tempting for researchers and practitioners to overlook or pay too little attention to the implications, impact and lessons of the full picture of a child's and family's experiences. Public interventions in their lives are only responses to some aspects of what goes on from day to day. For those who carry the responsibility for conducting such interventions these current aspects are of central concern; for the children and their families other things will be important as well.

The tendency for social workers to concentrate upon the present is accentuated because they do not generally remain responsible for a child in care or their family over long periods. The turnover of staff inevitably fragments the official record of a child's career. It was plain from the time that it took us thoroughly to read and digest the material on file that social workers must face major problems in acquainting themselves with the recorded history. Even then there may be gaps in what is available and some important matters will simply not have been written down.

Not only is there a need for records to contain accurate, up-to-date and readily accessible accounts of each child's care history but also for the statistics that are collected nationally to place greater emphasis upon data about 'careers'. That principle, of course, should be extended to their families as well; but its application to them is even more difficult. First it is difficult because there is no tradition of systematically collecting information about the families of children in care (for example, about how many have brothers or sisters in care with them or whether, on leaving care, they go back to the same household from which they came). The second reason for the difficulty is that the 'family' is by no means a fixed entity. Especially for children in care its membership is often volatile and significant members (from the child's point of view) come and go in ways and at a rate that make it hard for social workers to keep track. In that sense what may seem to be a stable setting for a child (because they do not move households) may actually be most unstable in terms of its fluctuating membership. Likewise, what may appear to be an unstable situation because of a child's movements from place to place may actually be relatively stable if, for example, it occurs within a large local extended family. It is obvious indeed that stability of place should not be confused with stability of relationships or vicinity.

The importance of paying attention to children's care careers was particularly highlighted by the findings about restoring Protected children. The chances of successful return were diminished when children had been subjected to placement changes in care or had prolonged experiences of separation from their families. Where the histories of either Protected or Disaffected children showed a previous failed restoration placement, the chances of successful reunion were much reduced.

Permanence

There has been little discussion of home on trial placements in the debates about permanence and permanence planning. This is a startling omission when we consider that the Oregon Project[10] in the United States, which played a leading role in developing the concept of permanence, made the restoration of children to their birth families the first permanence choice. However, in this country there has been only a slow development of the idea that permanence could include children's permanent re-unification with the family from which they had been separated.[11] This may have reflected the fact that the very idea of a 'trial' implied a probationary status which, by definition, could not be regarded as secure or permanent. At most it could be considered to be a prelude to permanence. Yet, as we have seen, many of the placements continued on this impermanent basis for long periods. There were also a few cases where a home on trial placement was used in order to demonstrate or confirm that restoration to a parent would not work and therefore that a permanent alternative should be sought. It was clear from our interviews with parents that some of them certainly felt that they lived under that shadow.

This was not surprising, for the continuing existence of a care order implies doubt and uncertainty. Yet our study suggests that in a sizeable proportion of the cases being home on trial is tantamount to permanent restoration. Where this is so then perhaps steps should be taken earlier to have the order discharged, albeit that either voluntary or mandatory support continues thereafter. The fact that that is felt to be needed should not be allowed to signal an extension of the trial under another name, any more than the emerging post-adoption services do. Indeed, the explicit recognition that problems and difficulties remain may well protect the child (and the family) from the collapse of an arrangement that is intended to be permanent.

The parents or carers of children home on trial need to know where they stand. That means that they should know what is expected of them and whether, subject to these conditions, it is the intention of a social services department to see their parental rights and duties fully restored. In that sense, it seems to us that the 'trial' element of these placements should become more explicit and its implications clearly and precisely explained to parents as well as to children where they are of an age to appreciate what is involved. For that to happen, however, it is essential for the 'trial' criteria to be set realistically; realistically in the sense that if conditions fail to be met it would be reasonable for the sanction of removal to be invoked. There is, we believe, a danger that for understandable reasons, social workers shy away from such action; but by being firmer about removal in the minority of instances where that is necessary it may become easier to proceed more confidently to establish the permanence of other placements.

There is also a danger that for want of decisive action some children home on trial remain there in what amounts to a permanently unsatisfactory condition. Some of our most telling evidence concerns the unlikelihood of a placement being successful if it has already been tried before with the same carers without success unless, that is, significant changes have occurred in the meantime. This raises the question of when and in what way permanent alternative care should be sought for children whose placements at home have been detrimental. There was little evidence from our study that this was seriously contemplated for more than a small number of these cases.

However, that said, we must again draw attention to the different implications that this would have for the younger Protected children and the older Disaffected group. In particular, there is the question of what permanency planning means for sixteen or seventeen-year-olds. The impermanence of a local authority's responsibility for them is soon to be realised as they reach their eighteenth birthdays.[12] It is plain that for many of these youngsters who were already adolescent when they were committed to care the extended family plays an important part in their lives. It is also clear from their actions that it is within this network that most of them wish to find a place. That being so, as we have argued earlier, more attention should be paid by departments to working with that larger family group. The question remains, however, of how far similar strategies could be used in a preventive fashion. It is tempting to conclude that they could and should. However, we remain cautious about the wider application of this principle for two reasons. First, because the circumstances of our two groups were so different and secondly because some of the youngsters in the Disaffected group, being older, were able to use their rotation within the wider family as a means of dealing with conflicts. They often did so in a way that would be hard for social workers to orchestrate for younger children.

Procedures

Our results include information about most of the procedures that were associated both with making home on trial decisions and with the subsequent social work that was undertaken. There was considerable variation between the authorities and between different cases. It is common to assume that tighter procedures lead to better results, and certainly the study offered some evidence to support that view. The problem however comes in trying to unravel cause and effect. As we noted earlier, it is unclear (at least from our work) what it is that is particularly valuable about this or that procedure. What, for example, does the full and regular completion of six-monthly reviews imply?

It could mean several things. First, it could reflect good management control over the conduct of cases. That, in its turn, might also be associated with good supervision and the availability of consultation. Secondly, a properly undertaken review is likely to provide an opportunity for assessment and reassessment as well as for planning what needs to be done next. Thirdly, the fact that certain cases (even within a local authority area) are more thoroughly reviewed than others may tell us something about the differential quality of the social work or management. Alternatively, the failure to complete regular six-monthly reviews might be accounted for by the fact that work on some cases is accorded lower priority than on others, either because they are not thought to be problematic (or no crisis has arisen) or because they are so difficult (say with wilful and elusive adolescents) that the exercise is regarded as a waste of time. Additionally, of course, whether or not reviews get done may depend upon the general level of pressure and morale in a department.

In these senses, therefore, procedures must be seen as indicators of other influential factors as well as having an influence of their own. That makes it difficult to disentangle their independent effect, especially when there may be the cross-cutting complication of some being followed more in the letter than in the spirit.

The introduction of regulations offers a good opportunity for the impact of new procedures to be assessed. We hope that encouragement will be given for this to be done. Of course, procedures can degenerate into sterile bureaucracy and, as a result, be circumvented or ignored by social workers as irrelevant burdens; but they can also be a valuable expression of responsibility and concern for accountability. Not least they are important means by which it becomes possible to monitor what is happening.

Differences between the Authorities

In both the Protected and Disaffected groups the profiles of the children and their careers were similar in the four authorities, and there were few differences in the kinds of households to which they returned or in the events during their time home on trial. In particular, there was no significant difference in terms of the outcomes at the end of our follow-up period or in relation to our evaluations of the placements. This may be thought to be a somewhat surprising finding, especially as there were certain differences in the procedures and practices of the four authorities. However, several factors need to be borne in mind before concluding that whatever local authorities do in this respect makes little difference to what happens to children who are home on trial.

First, it may be that procedural variations are not a good indicator of either the amount or appropriateness of the resources that are devoted to the support of children home on trial and their families. Secondly, we were unable to do more than calculate the frequency of, say, reviews or social work contacts. Had it been possible to examine what was done in more detail, differences in practice might have emerged which were related to different outcomes. Thirdly, we were conscious that there were often sharp differences between areas within departments and these may have cancelled each other out in the process of aggregating the data for each authority. A much bigger sample would have been needed in order to have been able to take this issue properly into account. As authorities adopt more localised systems of administration (which had happened in three of the four authorities) so the opportunities for internal variations in practice increase, as well as the need to have larger and larger research samples if these differences are to be detected and understood. Finally, of course, we selected our four authorities because they were close to the national average in terms of their use of home on trial. It is possible that this excluded authorities with more divergent practices which could have affected the pattern of outcomes.

A Final Comment

Child care is at a cross-roads. New ways ahead are being pioneered. New standards are being expected and sought. The Children Act heralds the most far-reaching reform of child care law since 1969, if not since 1948. High standards of social work practice with children and families now exist (as our study made clear) albeit that achievement is uneven. It would be a sad matter if children who in the past have been classed as being home on trial were to be left behind by these developments. It would be sadder still if we failed to restore children to their parents when that could be done without endangering their wellbeing. Saddest of all would be our failure to prevent children being committed to care who did not need to be subject to such drastic intervention. Our study must at least place something of a question mark over that issue, given the relatively high rate of 'successful' placements back home that the results revealed.

Notes and references

1. This issue is discussed more fully in R. A. Parker, *A Forward Look at Research on the Child in Care*, Bristol Papers in Applied Social Studies, No.2, School of Applied Social Studies, University of Bristol, 1987.
2. Charge and Control regulations, *op. cit.*
3. *Ibid*, section 8.
4. For a full commentary on the Act see White, Carr and Lowe, *op. cit.*
5. *Accommodation of Children with Parents etc. (Guidance and Control Regulations)*, 1990, *op. cit.*
6. *Ibid*, p. 4.
7. *Ibid*, p. 10.
8. *Ibid*, p. 15.
9. For a brief review of the evidence see Berridge and Cleaver, *op. cit.*, introduction.
10. V. Pike (1976), *op. cit.*
11. However Thoburn, amongst others, has emphasised this important aspect of 'permanence'; see her 'What Kind of Permanence?', *Adoption and Fostering*, vol. 9, no. 4, 1985, and also J. Thoburn, A Murdoch and A. O'Brian, *Permanence in Child Care*, Blackwell, 1986.
12. Albeit that, in certain circumstances, the Children Act, 1989 allows local authorities to extend help and supervision until the young person reaches 21.

Appendix

Appendix

The Statistical Analysis

In this study we have sought to identify factors which would help social workers to recognise children who are or are not vulnerable to problems in their 'home on trial' placement. We do not offer hard and fast tests which social workers can follow with total confidence but rather suggest guidelines and checklists which can aid decision-making. Nonetheless, we have subjected our data to rigorous testing.

At the outset, several difficulties had to be overcome but three problems were pressing. First, we had to find a way of disentangling the relationship between associated variables using a method applicable to categorical data which made up the majority of information collected from the files. Secondly, we were concerned to identify multi-collinearity, that is, when two variables are so closely related to each other that there are dangers in treating them as separate entities in any statistical analysis. Thirdly, we were aware that individual cases with unusual characteristics may lead to misleading findings. In order to deal with these problems the following procedure was applied to the data.

Initially, we had to select the important variables which may individually or in combination predict known outcomes. We used knowledge built up during the collection of the information in order to select a manageable group of variables: for example, conversations with social workers; the analysis of the interviews with social workers and parents who had current or recent experience of a home on trial placement; and lessons learned in the review of relevant literature. This group of variables was then subjected to the relatively simple exercise of cross-tabulating the possible carriers (also known as independent variables) with the response (or dependent) variable; that is, whether or not the home on trial had a satisfactory outcome.

In the cross-tabulation exercises, different measures of association were used depending upon whether the data were ordinal, nominal, categorical or continuous. For instance, in testing the association between two truly dichotomous variables the *phi* co-efficient was used.[1]

The knowledge acquired during the study, together with the cross-tabulation exercises, helped us to reduce the number of carriers to about 15 for each of our two main groups. Not all of these variables were significantly associated with the response variable: some were included because we felt that they would be important in combination with other factors. In order to look more rigorously at such associations, we produced correlation matrices of the response and carriers using Goodman and Kruskal's *gamma* to test the power of relationships. This procedure also reduced the likelihood of multi-collinearity.

We next selected those variables which, in combination with each other, were most likely to predict the greatest proportion of children experiencing a known outcome. Before we tested this proposition, we also checked the data for outliers; that is to say individual cases which may cause a change in the statistical line of fit and produce misleading results. Outliers were identified using computer programmes to detect outlying members of groups based on presence-absence data[2] and by scrutiny of the frequency distribution of the various combination of variables.

Finally, we tested the relationship between the carriers and response variables using log-linear techniques. This approach has been developed to test the relationship between different parts of complex multi-way tables, for example, those produced when four variables are cross-tabulated.[3] For the purposes of the 'home on trial' analysis, we were interested in whether or not there was a relationship between dependent and independent variables and thus used a special type of log-linear analysis known as logit.[4] Logit turns the actual outcome variable, for instance 0 (negative outcome to placement) and 1 (positive outcome to placement) into 'log odds' which, put simply, is a calculation based upon the number of times an event occurs divided by the number of times it does not occur.

The calculations involved in such analysis are lengthy and time-consuming but there are numerous statistical packages available to undertake the work, most notably GLIM, SPSSX and BMDP. We used SPSSX because it gives the widest range of statistics and the computer output produces co-efficients which can be used as a check upon interpretation. Thus we managed to keep total control of all of the complex statistical tasks undertaken.

Those wishing to have more detailed information about this methodology should contact Dr M. Little, Dartington Social Research Unit, Foxhole, Dartington, Totnes, Devon.

Notes and references

1. L. Cohen and M. Holliday, *Statistics for Social Scientists*, Harper and Row, 1982.
2. P.H.A. Sneath and C.D. Langham, 'Outlier: a basic program for detecting outlying members of multi-variate clusters based on presence-absence data', *Computers and Geosciences*, vol. 15, no. 6, 1989.
3. S.L. Haberman, *Analysis of Qualitative Data: Volume 1, Introductory Topics*, Academic Press, New York, 1978.
4. D. Knoke and P. J. Burke, *Log-Linear Models*, Sage, Beverley Hill, 1980.

Bibliography

Aldgate J. (1977), *The Identification of Factors Influencing Children's Length of Stay in Care*, Ph.D. thesis, University of Edinburgh.

Berridge D. and Cleaver H (1987), *Foster Home Breakdown*, Blackwell.

British Association of Social Workers (1980), *Clients are Fellow Citizens*, BASW.

Brown C. (1984), *Child Abuse Parents Speaking: A Consumer Study*, School for Advanced Urban Studies, Working Paper 63, University of Bristol.

Bullard E. and Malos E. (1991, forthcoming), *Custodianship: Caring for Other People's Children*, HMSO.

Butler-Sloss (1988), *Report of the Inquiry into Child Abuse in Cleveland 1987*, Cm.412, HMSO.

Carlebach J. (1970), *Caring for Children in Trouble*, Routledge and Kegan Paul.

Cawson P. (n.d.), *Young Offenders in Care*, Social Research Branch, DHSS.

Cawson P. (1987). 'The Sexist Social Worker? Some Gender Issues in Social Work Practice with Adolescent Girls', *Practice*, 1.

Central Statistical Office (1984), *Social Trends 14*, HMSO.

Children's Legal Centre (1981), *Evidence to the NISW Committee*.

Children's Legal Centre (1984), *It's My Life, Not Theirs*.

Cohen L. and Holliday M. (1982), *Statistics for Social Scientists*, Harper and Row.

Cooper R. A. (1982, unpublished), *A Study of Children 'Trial-Own-Parent' Subjects of Care Orders under the 1969 Children and Young Persons Act in Sheffield*.

Crittenden P. (1988), 'Family Dyadic Patterns of Functioning in Maltreating Families' in Browne K., Davies C., and Stratton P. (eds.), *Early Prediction and Prevention of Child Abuse*, Wiley and Sons.

Curtis Report (1946), *Report of the Care of Children Committee*, Cmd.6922, HMSO.

Dale P. (1986), *Dangerous Families: Assessment and Treatment of Child Abuse*, Tavistock.

Dartington Social Research Unit (1984), *Place of Safety Orders: A Study of Children Provided for Under Section 28 of the Children and Young Persons Act, 1969;* Research Report.

Dartington Social Research Unit (1984), *Predicting Children's Length of Stay in Care and the Relevance of Family Links;* Research Report.

Department of Health (1989), *An Introduction to the Children Act, 1989,* HMSO.

Department of Health (1990), The Children Act, 1989, Consultation Paper no. 9, *Accommodation of Children with Parents etc. (Guidance and Control Regulations)*.

DHSS (1981), *A Study of the Boarding-Out of Children*, Social Work Service.

DHSS (1982), *Child Abuse: A Study of Inquiry Reports 1973-1981*, HMSO.

DHSS (1985), *Children in the Care of Local Authorities for the Year Ending 31 March, 1984, England*.

DHSS (1986), *Children in Care in England and Wales, March 1984*, HMSO.

DHSS, Social Services Inspectorate (1985), *Inspection of Community Homes.*

DHSS, Social Services Inspectorate (1986), *Inspection of the Supervision of Social Workers in the Assessment and Monitoring of Cases of Child Abuse when Children Subject to a Court Order have been Returned Home.*

DHSS, Social Services Inspectorate (1988), *Inspection of Cleveland Social Services Department's Arrangements for Handling Child Sexual Abuse.*

Department of Health, Social Services Inspectorate (1990), *Child Care Policy: Putting it in Writing. A Review of English Local Authorities' Child Care Policy Statements*, HMSO.

Department of Health and Welsh Office (1989), *Handbook of Guidance: Charge and Control Placements.*

DHSS and Welsh Office (1988), *Working Together: A Guide to Inter-Agency Co-operation for the Protection of Children from Abuse*, HMSO.

Dingwall R., Eekelaar J. and Murray R. (1983), *The Protection of Children*, Blackwell.

Essex Area Review Committee (1981), *Malcolm Page*, Essex County Council.

Family Rights Group (1981), *The Three R's of Social Work*, a submission to the National Institute for Social Work Inquiry.

Fanshel D. (1975), 'Parental Visiting of Children in Foster Care: Key to Discharge?' in *Social Services Review*, vol. 49, no. 4.

Fanshel D. (1976), 'Status Changes of Children in Foster Care: Final Results of the Columbia University Longitudinal Study', in *Child Welfare*, vol. 55, no. 3.

Farmer E. and Parker R. A. (1985), *A Study of Interim Care Orders*, Department of Social Administration, University of Bristol.

Farmer E. and Parker R. A. (1985), *A Study of the Discharge of Care Orders*, Department of Social Administration, University of Bristol.

Fein E., Maluccio, A. N., Hamilton J. and Ward D. E. (1983), 'After Foster Care: Permanency Planning for Children', in *Child Welfare*, 62(6).

Fisher M., Marsh P., Phillips D. and Sainsbury E. (1986), *In and Out of Care: The Experiences of Children, Parents and Social Workers*, Batsford.

George V. (1970), *Foster Care: Theory and Practice*, Routledge and Kegan Paul.

Gottesfeld H. (1970), *In Loco Parentis: A Study of Perceived Role Values in Foster Home Care*, Jewish Welfare Association, New York.

Haberman S. L. (1978), *Analysis of Qualitative Data: Volume 1, Introductory Topics*, Academic Press, New York.

Hazel N. (1981), *A Bridge to Independence*, Blackwell.

Hensey O. J., Williams J. K. and Rosenbloom L. (1983), 'Intervention in Child Abuse: Experience in Liverpool', in *Developmental Medicine and Child Neurology*, 25.

Home Office (1961), *Eighth Report on the Work of the Children's Department*, HMSO.

Jackson S. (1987), *The Education of Children in Care*, Bristol Papers in Applied Social Studies, No. 1, University of Bristol.

Knapp M *et al.* (1985), *The Objectives of Child Care and Their Attainment Over a Twelve Month Period for a Cohort of New Admissions: the Suffolk Cohort Study*, Discussion Paper 373, Personal Social Services Research Unit, University of Kent.

Knoke D. and Burke P. J. (1980), *Log-Linear Models*, Sage, Beverley Hills.

Lahti J. (1982), 'A Follow-Up Study of Foster Children In Permanent Placements', in *Social Service Review*, 56(4).

London Borough of Brent (1985), *A Child in Trust: The Report of the Panel of Inquiry into the Circumstances Surrounding the Death of Jasmine Beckford*.

London Borough of Lambeth (1987), *Whose Child? The Report of the Panel Appointed to Inquire into the Death of Tyra Henry*.

Lowe N. and White R. (1979), _Wards of Court_, Butterworths.

Lynch M. A. and Roberts J. (1982), _The Consequences of Child Abuse_, Academic Press.

Maluccio A. N., Fein E. and Olmstead K. A. (1986), _Permanency Planning for Children: Concepts and Methods_, Tavistock.

Millham S., Bullock R., Hosie K. and Haak M. (1986), _Lost in Care: the Problems of Maintaining Links Between Children in Care and their Families_, Gower.

Morrison T. (1987), 'Creating Changes in Abusing Families' in _Adoption and Fostering_, vol. 11, no. 2.

Murch M. and Mills L. (1987), _The Length of Care Proceedings_, Socio-Legal Centre for Family Studies, University of Bristol.

National Association for the Care and Resettlement of Offenders (1988), _Grave Crimes, Grave Doubts_.

National Council for One Parent Families (1981), _Inquiry into Social Work—Evidence to the NISW Committee_.

Packman J. (1986), _Who Needs Care? Social Work Decisions About Children_, Blackwell.

Parker R. A. (1966), _Decision in Child Care_, Allen and Unwin.

Parker R. A. (1985), 'Planning into Practice', in _Adoption and Fostering_, vol. 9, no. 4.

Parker R. A. (1987), _A Forward Look at Research on the Child in Care_, Bristol Papers in Applied Social Studies, No. 2, School of Applied Social Studies, University of Bristol.

Parker R. A. (1988), 'Children', in Sinclair I. (ed.), _Residential Care: The Research Reviewed_, vol. II (Wagner Report), HMSO.

Parker R. A. (1991), _Away From Home: A Short History of Provision for Separated Children_, Barnardos.

Pike V. (1976), 'Permanency Planning for Foster Children: the Oregon Project', in *Children Today*, 5(6).

Power M. J. *et al.* (1974), 'Delinquency and the Family', *British Journal of Social Work*, no. 4.

Quinton D. and Rutter M. (1988), *Parenting Breakdown: The Making and Breaking of Inter-Generational Links*, Avebury.

Rose G. (1967), *Schools for Young Offenders*, Tavistock.

Rowe J. and Lambert L. (1973), *Children Who Wait*, Association of British Adoption Agencies.

Rowe J., Hundleby M. and Garnett L. (1989), *Child Care Now: A Survey of Placement Patterns*, British Agencies for Adoption and Fostering.

Rushton A., Treseder J. and Quinton D. (1988), *New Parents for Older Children*, British Agencies for Adoption and Fostering.

Simpson L. (1981), *What Happens to Children in Care? A Report on Children in Care in Lambeth*, Lambeth Social Services Department.

Sinclair R. (1984), *Decision Making in Statutory Reviews in Children in Care*, Gower.

Sinclair R. (1987), *Children Home on Trial in Leicestershire*, Leicestershire Social Services Department, Research Section.

Sinclair R. (1988), 'Recording Social Work Objectives', in *Research, Policy and Planning*, vol. 5, no. 2.

Sneath P. H. A. and Langham C. D. (1989), 'Outlier: a basic program for detecting outlying members of multi-variate clusters based on presence-absence data', *Computers and Geosciences*, vol. 15, no. 6.

Stein M. and Carey K. (1986), *Leaving Care*, Blackwell.

Stevenson O. and Smith J. (1983), *Report of the Implementation of Section 56 of the Children Act, 1975*, Department of Social Policy and Social Work, University of Keele.

Thoburn J. (1980), *Captive Clients: Social Work with Families of Children Home on Trial*, Routledge and Kegan Paul.

Thoburn J. (1985), 'What Kind of Permanence?', *Adoption and Fostering*, vol. 9, no. 4.

Thoburn J., Murdoch A. and O'Brian A. (1986), *Permanence in Child Care*, Blackwell.

Tipler J. (1986), *Juvenile Justice in Hackney*, Hackney Social Services Department.

Trasler G. (1960), *In Place of Parents*, Routledge and Kegan Paul.

Vernon J. and Fruin D. (1986), *In Care: A Study of Social Work Decision Making*, National Children's Bureau.

West D. J. and Farrington D. P. (1977), *The Delinquent Way of Life*, Heinemann.

White R., Carr P. and Lowe N. (1990), *A Guide to the Children Act, 1989*, Butterworths.

Wolkind S. (1988), *The Mental Health of Children in Care—Research Needs*, Economic and Social Research Council.

Zander M. (1975), 'What Happens to Young Offenders in Care', in *New Society*, 24 July.

Printed in the United Kingdom for HMSO
Dol. 292968 C20 7/91